Conversation Piece

Collection Mu.ZEE Ostend
Acquisitions 2007–2012

Content

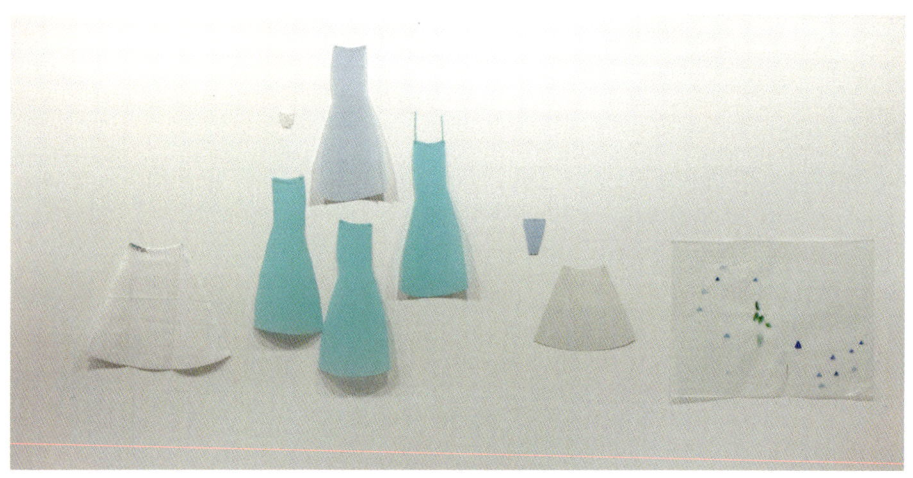

Guy Mees, *Imaginair ballet*, 1998

Conversation Piece

PHILLIP VAN DEN BOSSCHE IN CONVERSATION WITH MIEKE MELS
ABOUT THE Mu.ZEE COLLECTION

Mieke Mels: The museum's mission is to build a unique collection of Belgian art from 1850 to the present. What are the considerations that surround collection building today? What informs the choices made and which criteria are followed?

Phillip Van den Bossche: The creation of a framework is very important. A content-related framework should function autonomously and be checked against the various criteria formulated in the collection plan. There is a choice of possible trajectories and side-tracks that connect with the outside world — ranging from exhibitions and temporary loans to collaborations with other collections — but a good basic structure ensures both the existence of a framework and the possibility to look beyond it. They reinforce each other.

First of all, you never start from scratch. You always build on the history of the collection, both in terms of its origin as in the way it has grown (organically or otherwise) over the years. It appears that there are a number of important gaps in the historically grown collection(s) of Mu.ZEE. The sixties, seventies and eighties are underrepresented. I am thinking of the work of Lili Dujourie, Jan Vercruysse and Guy Mees. Of course, these gaps are offset by very well-developed periods, with key figures such as James Ensor and Léon Spilliaert, and the modernism of the twenties and thirties. One of our main focus points remains the acquisition of new 'historical' works, conditions on the art market permitting. In addition, the number of female artists is underrepresented in the collection. This has become one of the issues, but does not imply that works are bought because they are made by a female artist. Gender is not a decisive argument but concrete figures notwithstanding, it is clear that a start has been made to counter this disproportion. In parallel, attention is also paid to the underrepresentation of video and multimedia in the collection.

Perhaps one of the most important criteria is the strict limitation to Belgian art. The museum has always adhered to this and this position is also continued today.
With regard to its acquisition policy, the museum has always focused on Belgian art, but has, in terms of exhibitions, always functioned on an international level. I think this is an interesting starting point. It has to do with a certain consciousness, a form of modesty and relativism that is becoming increasingly relevant. The available resources are limited, but—perhaps more importantly—one is aware that it is impossible to collect everything. The focus on Belgian art is in this sense a meaningful limitation that opens possibilities to create connections in different ways and further expand the collection, even if only temporarily or indirectly. Since 2008, Mu.ZEE has been collecting artists who live and work in Belgium. An artist is never isolated. He is embedded in a community, which is a determining factor… The idea that this approach can be applied retroactively is an attractive given; it can be extended to artists who have lived and worked in Belgium, either for a long or short time. This retrospective aspect is useful because, as an institute, we have to guard against becoming an 'island' of Belgian art. This would create a very artificial image that is inconsistent with the reality in which artists move, travel…

In what way does this translate into the reality of the museum? What strategies are used in this context?
In the first place, the acquisition policy is framed within the context of the broader museum operation. To think about the collection is to think about the museum as a whole. It is the starting point from which other lines are defined—exhibitions, collection presentations, public activities. Irrespective of the size of the purchasing budget, the starting point is always the artist and the collection, and through collaborations with private collectors and other public institutions, opportunities are created that allow us to present a broader picture to the public and involve the international community. To give an example: *Belgian Blues* (1990) is a work by Thomas Schütte, part of the collection of S.M.A.K., but since 2010 entrusted to Mu.ZEE as a long-term loan. This work is an important element in our approach to the collection, and for several reasons. First and foremost, Schütte created this installation

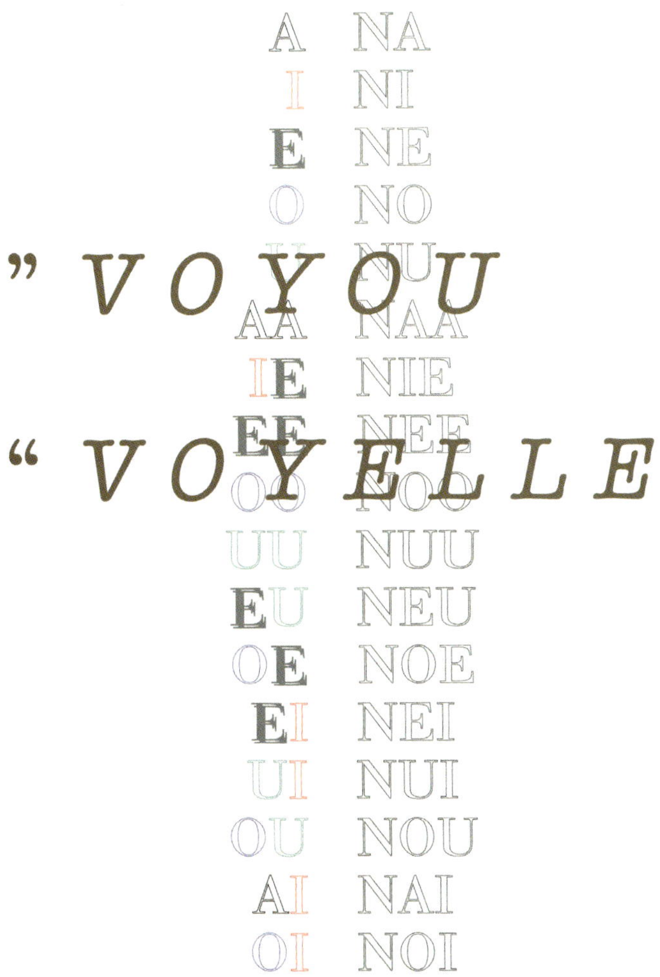

Jan Vercruysse, *Les Consonants*, 2010–11

in Ostend and there is a direct link with the sea in the work. But on a visual level, the artist—and more specifically the work—relates to artists and contemporaries like Jan Vercruysse and Lili Dujourie, who take a central place in the museum's acquisition policy.

During a lecture at a club of private collectors in Bruges, Chris Dercon, director of Tate Modern, indicated that the general public is no longer interested (and perhaps never was interested) in the specification 'private collection' or 'on loan from' marked on the title cards in the exhibition space. If you think about this, you can conclude two things: either a museum should stop collecting, a line of thought which I do not agree with because then you stop being a museum altogether; or you can deal with collection development in a flexible manner, for instance through collaborations and temporary collection relationships (however, always with an eye on the expansion of the museum collection). Here, we can cite the example of *Passion #1* and *Passion #2*, in which a dialogue was created between two Belgian collections, the Mu.ZEE and the Belfius collection, an art collection of over 4,500 works. Both collections complement each other. One possible reaction would be to put everything in motion to acquire this collection and create one large, overarching whole. The 'owning', however, has become irrelevant and this is exactly what Dercon points out. A temporary dialogue, as such, is a much more interesting way to reflect upon one's own collection.

The approach to the collection is always shaped through a dialogue with the artists whose work we purchase. I enter into dialogue with them

about other artists they find interesting. In the process, they reveal a
small part of their frame of reference or give insight into their community.
The acquisitions of the last six years clearly illustrate this development.
We do not build a collection of singular pieces with artworks functioning
as separate islands. We collect on the basis of 'thinking in terms of
ensembles'. Several works of a particular artist are purchased and a relationship of trust is forged over the years. Sometimes this dialogue
leads to interesting donations. We travel a journey together.

In 2012, I bought a complete exhibition by Jos de Gruyter & Harald Thys,
Objects as Friends (2011), which was on view at Mu.ZEE in the summer
of that year. It includes more than 300 photographs. I could have made
a selection but instead acquired the series as a whole. This targeted
acquisition also suggests international influences, with references to
artists like Isa Genzken and Peter Fischli & David Weiss. I approached
the work of Ann Veronica Janssens in a similar way. *Riffs* (2008) is a video
installation that contains thirteen videos. By purchasing it as a whole,
one of the artist's fields of investigation was kept entirely intact, which
created opportunities to investigate various presentation possibilities
in dialogue with the artist (cf. *Passion # 2,* ed.).

A number of directions are possible. A choice can be made for a key
work in a certain oeuvre. In 2007, for instance, I bought *TOMBEAUX* (1987)
by Jan Vercruysse, an important work in his oeuvre. To my surprise,
I learned that this was the first sculpture from the *TOMBEAUX* series to end
up in a Belgian public collection. In other words, with this purchase,
I did not just fill a gap in our own collection. Or a more transitional work,
one that heralds an evolution toward a different type of work, could be
chosen. We acquired, for instance, Lili Dujourie's *Crépuscule* (1985);
a work considered pivotal by the artist herself. It is from the period in

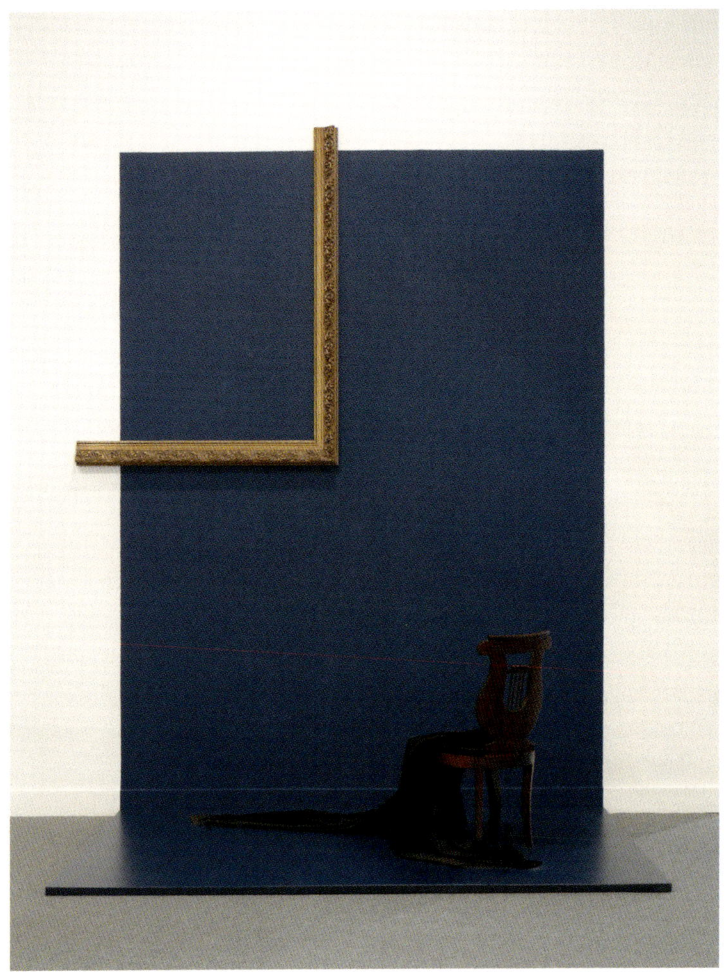

Lili Dujourie, *Crépuscule*, 1985

which she worked on the boundary between wall and floor. It is also interesting to select a *Fremdkörper,* a work that doesn't quite fit. Once one or more works of a particular artist have been acquired, it becomes important to reflect on how a new purchase will relate to those works. Is it a supplement or does it represent a different aspect of that artist? In this way, for example, I purchased Lili Dujourie's slide series *Oostende* (1974), a brilliant masterpiece. Obviously the location played a role here as well, but apart from that, this truly belongs in the Mu.ZEE collection and fills an important gap.

To what extent does your own subjectivity affect your collecting for a public institution, despite the framework that has obviously been put in place?

When I consider the way collection building was approached until recently—and that is part of my background as well—I can see how even in public collections this was strongly driven by subjective arguments that were for the most part inspired by the museum director. The presence of a buying commission was in most cases of trivial importance. In 1999, the Van Abbemuseum published the book *Een collectie is ook maar een mens (A Collection is Only Human).* It contains interviews with four successive directors about their purchasing policy—Edy de Wilde (1946–1963), Jean Leering (1964–1973), Rudi Fuchs (1975–1987) and Jan Debbaut (1988–2003). The title of the book says it all… Recently, I have been wondering whether this subjective approach still exists today. Is there is no objective framework that could bridge the gap between the subjective and the objective?

Collecting is making choices, but doesn't making choices also mean missing out on things?

It is interesting to consider that question from the artist's point of view. Today, it has indeed become difficult for an artist to create art. Until well into the twentieth century, there was a consensus on the production of art and the fact that it could, as it were, be placed on a line, like a chain of subsequent reactions. Later, structuralism and postmodernism expertly dismantled this chronological image. The Canadian artist Jeff Wall asserts that today it is no longer evident to make art because there is no more foundation from which to build a body of work: 'the conditions to make art are suspended.' Wall can link his photographs to the seventeenth century and the origin of photography. He can, in other words, mark off a line, but today this has become virtually impossible. An interesting example is the work of Michael Van den Abeele. I have purchased three of his paintings, although he himself feels he is not a painter. Still, he paints and to me this illustrates the loss of foundations from which an artist can operate. Artists whose work I think should be bought by a museum—which is of course always somewhat of a subjective given—are artists who seek solutions to that fundamental problem. What are the foundations that underlie my work? What is their significance in art historical terms?

The medium is no longer a foundation. The idea prevails and the manner in which it is executed is to be examined work by work.

Indeed. At the end of 2012, we presented the exhibition *Vinyl in the Studio. Artists' Record Sleeves in Belgium.* The reason I wanted to do this is precisely because it does not matter in which medium an idea is captured. This is a valuable legacy of the Conceptual art from the sixties and seventies. Unfortunately, the medium is still the basis for most art teaching in Belgium. John Baldessari for example, gave a very different message to the students at the California Institute of the Arts. The medium is not important. You start training as a painter and you graduate for example as someone who makes music. It becomes a matter of and / and: you write a poetry book and make a painting and a sculpture… meantime you quickly design a poster for your friends' gig. Here, this way of thinking and acting is given far too little attention.

In 2011, the German philosopher Diedrich Diederichsen wrote *Radicalism as Ego Ideal: Oedipus and Narcissus,* a text which I think bridges the gap between contemporary art and Jeff Wall's view. Artists no longer follow the straight line of art history, but create their own genealogy. Diederichsen talks about a paradigm shift. Older generations of artists were caught in an action / reaction Oedipus complex. The current generation of artists has shifted toward the realm of Narcissus. They no longer feel the need to 'kill' their teachers but build their own community of 'related' artists, and create something new based on this micro-world. I see this as a positive way of thinking about individualism, which is usually pejoratively understood as: they are only preoccupied with themselves. What is positive, however, is the decision to select, as an artist, which elements in (art) history are interesting. Someone like Koenraad Dedobbeleer builds his own frame of reference which branches out from Adolf Loos to Manfred Pernice. In his work, he questions the contemporaneity of the work of Robert Morris, couples this to an interest in a designer such as Achille Castiglione, or Memphis

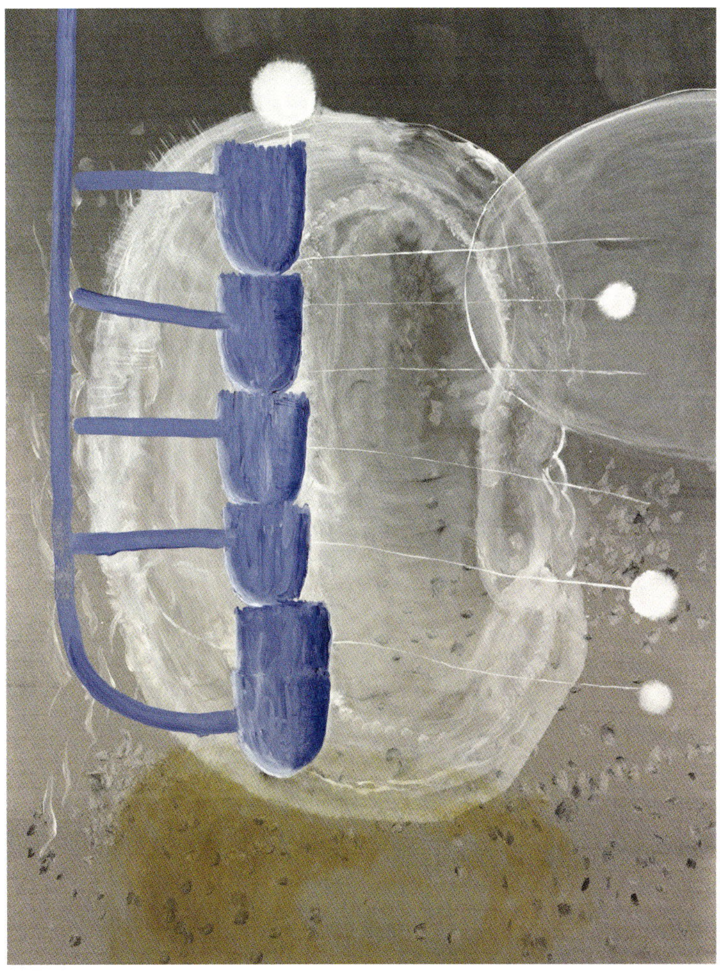

Michael Van den Abeele, *Blauwe Blisters,* 2010

postmodernism, and the in art circles widely acclaimed and polemical work of Ettore Sottsass, for example. I find it immensely interesting to apply this approach to the collection.

An artist creates his own genealogy, and can, without having to justify himself, make connections and decide what is important. Mu.ZEE collects both modern and contemporary art. How can these two be brought together and ultimately lead to new insights that transcend particular time frames, genealogies or chronologies?
For me, there is a connection when we speak of idiosyncratic artists or artworks. I automatically think of artists such as Georges Vantongerloo or Jean Brusselmans. The latter is an artist who has always charted his own course and never really belonged to any artistic movement. He stood outside it all yet had a foot inside as well. I could also mention Jef Geys or Anne-Mie Van Kerckhoven. Their oeuvre functions as a world in itself. Their work deals with the *zeitgeist;* it is both a part of life and a commentary on it.

There were quite a few purchases of Jean Brusselmans' works at the time of the Mu.ZEE exhibition in 2011. Does an exhibition act as a catalyst for procurement, or is it rather the other way around?
Before an exhibition the size of *Jean Brusselmans* is publicly announced, preparations have been going on behind the scenes for a full two years. Whatever the circumstances, the moment the exhibition becomes a public event, works by the artist suddenly appear on the market at prices higher than before. So obviously, interesting purchases can be made in the fringes. No matter how small or large the acquisition budget is, it is always more interesting to stay away from the centre. If we would only focus on works that sell well or are popular on the market, we, as a public institution, would hardly be able to acquire anything seeing how we could never compete with the budget of private collectors. However, an interest in the periphery will often reveal a large number of intriguing artists and artworks that are currently not in the spotlight but might very well be in ten or twenty years.

Collecting also implies financial responsibility and being forced to function within a given market mechanism. To formulate priorities is one thing, but to execute them is another matter. To what extent does this affect the building of a collection of modern and contemporary works?

If you consider modern versus contemporary art, there is a difference. With a limited budget, works of contemporary artists can still be purchased, which, in case of some modern artists, is something one can only dream of. The focus should remain on the historical collection and the gaps and notable additions. I briefly mentioned it at the outset; it is still an important policy issue to find possible additions to the strong clusters in the collection. For the twenties and thirties, I think of works by Jozef Peeters, Paul Joostens, Jules Schmalzigaug and also Georges Vantongerloo. There are several paintings and a drawing by Vantongerloo in the collection. However, there are but few works of his on the market and prices are staggering. Still, this does not prevent me from keeping an interest in his work. It remains a benchmark in the Belgian art of the twentieth century.

The policy plan states the ambition to buy, whenever possible, works by key figures. Which works where you able to acquire within that context in the last six years?

Sometimes a purchase results from a chain of coincidences, and then grows into a policy issue. In 2008, I bought *Beachscape with Bathers* (1938) by Jean Brusselmans. I had just started in Mu.ZEE, and the acquisition budget was considerably lower than it is now. Since that first purchase, which made a serious dent in the budget, I have made it an issue to make a large purchase of art historical importance every year. After Brusselmans I purchased Léon Spilliaert's *Portrait de P.-G. Van Hecke et Norine* (1920) in 2009. This is a nice example of a *Fremdkörper* in his oeuvre that also reveals an important piece of Belgian art history. In 2011, I purchased the only known *Autoportrait* (1916) by Georges Vantongerloo, but I know all too well that purchases such as these will not always be possible, seeing how the prices for such major works are constantly rising. For me, the works by Brusselmans, Vantongerloo and Spilliaert together form an archipelago around which smaller works—drawings, watercolours, books…—can be clustered.

You already talked about the embedding of the collection policy in the museum as a whole, and the impact on temporary exhibitions, collection

Presenting the collection on the basis of various setups is a given that is continuously evolving. The presentation of collection pieces is like thinking aloud. Some presentations are successful, others I see as interesting 'failures'. Both are needed. In Flanders, issues pertaining to the collection (both in terms of education and public accessibility) are often reduced to conversations about quantity: the building of a warehouse and the provision of sufficient square footage to present the collection. Whatever the surface area of the museum may be, it does not change the percentage of collection items that can be displayed: on average 10 to 20%.

There is a trend toward making exhibitions in which works from private collections play a major role. This is readily dismissed as a result of the crisis and the ever increasing cost of loans and transports. Do you agree with this reasoning?

Of course this is true to a certain extent, but I think this also has to do with the growing number of freelance curators—a situation which was non-existent until recently, and originated somewhere in the early nineties. These freelancers explore uncharted territory through their work with the collections of various museums. They discover treasures in warehouses and make new connections. And this is why a good and professional warehouse is so important; it is the hardware of the museum.

Freelance curators explore various collections, but also work with them outside the museums. Think of the numerous biennials of contemporary art in which more and more historical art works are integrated to tell a larger story.

It is the task of a museum to tell stories, which is not the same as working in a narrative manner. More than ever, contemporary artists seek to connect with modern or ancient art. I just talked about the artist's quest for an individual genealogy, in which (art) history is rethought and reinterpreted. For us as a museum, this is an important and necessary task in these exciting times as well. On a social, political, economic and cultural level, we find ourselves on the brink of something new. The word 'change' is often mentioned, but nobody knows what exactly it will bring. It is no easy task, but as a museum we have an important social

and ideological mission. With exhibitions and collection presentations
we can create an ever-changing context; work together with artists
to bring transcendent values to the fore. The museum is a public space
where visitors get to make their own choices. To preserve art and
imagine a future through history is something we do together. In this
context, the new is inevitable. Think of the power of the *Ursonate*
by Kurt Schwitters, written between 1922 and 1932, and how the work
literally opens up a world, even today. I hope to realise the same for
the generations to come, through Jos de Gruyter & Harald Thys' photographs or the paintings of Jean Brusselmans. This is why the on-
going investment in a collection is also, indirectly, an investment in the
minds of people.

Thinking about the collection takes central place in the operation of
the museum, yet, at the same time, this can only be interesting when the
artist is heard. As a museum, we ultimately create our own genealogy,
composed of clusters and points of attention, without too rigid a structure. Artists show us how we can reclaim our freedom and how we
should use it. This is why the autonomy of art is so important. Camiel
van Winkel stated that very accurately, 'autonomy is precisely the cha-
racteristic in which art presents itself in its most social form.'[1] There is a
statement of the composer Wolfgang Rihm which I have often thought
about in the last months: 'It is for many, even culturally interested
people, hard to understand that harmony is not the absence of contradictions, but the presence of contradictions in a state in which the
components—like charges—keep each other in place.'[2] This could be
about us and it could very well be about the collection as well.

Ostend, 7 November 2012

1   Recorded in *Metropolis M,* August 2011.
2   Source: http://jefboven.blogspot.be/2012_08_01_archive.html.

KOENRAAD DEDOBBELEER

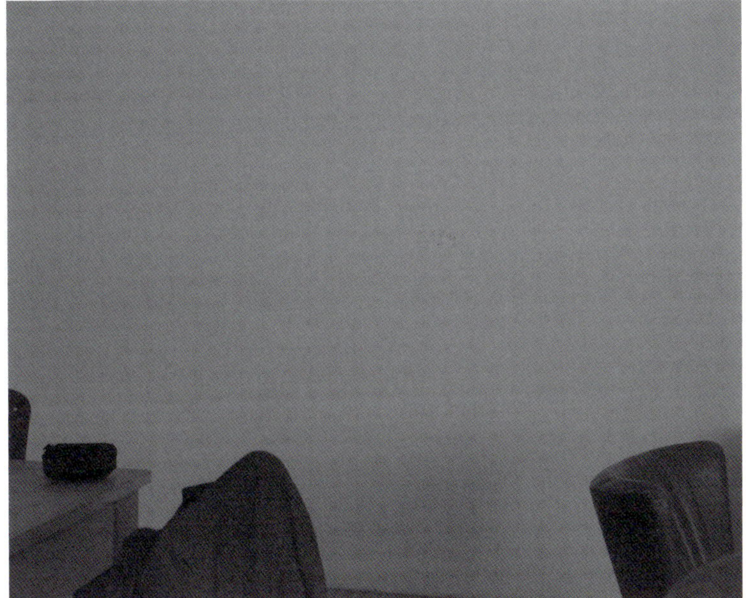

Oostende

2013

KOENRAAD DEDOBBELEER

du même auteur

Oostende

2013

Mu.ZEE – Kunstmuseum aan Zee

2008

Boredom Won't Starve as Long as I Feed It
Nürnberg, Verlag für Moderne Kunst
48 pp., 11 black and white photographs and 9 colour photographs
edition of 750 of which a certain number contains UP8

Explain It to the One Who Couldn't Care
Bruxelles, Gevaert Editions
24 pp., 18 colour photographs
edition of 30, signed and numbered

Dare Not Say: To Be Forgotten What to Say
Bruxelles, Gevaert Editions
two folded posters in a jacket
edition of 30, signed and numbered

Already Uttered on Numerous Occasions in Various Places
Bruxelles, Gevaert Editions
32 pp., 19 colour photographs
edition of 300

Based Less on Substance Than on Profit
Lisboa, Culturgest
80 pp., 59 colour photographs and 1 black and white photograph
edition of 300 of which 100 are signed and numbered

A Homemade Plan
Brussel, MOREpublishers
paper model in a jacket
edition of 25 + 5 A.P., signed and numbered

What You Carry in You, the Bastards Can't Touch
Barcelona, ProjecteSD
96 pp., 64 black and white photographs
edition of 200 of which 50 are signed and numbered

Doublure : catalogues d'expositions
Paris, &: Christophe Daviet-Thery
16 pp., in leporello, 2 colour photographs
edition of 300

Numerous Settlements for a Question
Bruxelles, Gevaert Editions
two books and two inkjet prints in a slipcase
edition of 30, signed and numbered

Space Has No Meaning Outside of Time
Paris, &: Christophe Daviet-Thery
18 pp., leporello, 11 black and white photographs in a jacket
edition of 200, signed and numbered

Ignorance Never Settles a Question
Antwerpen, Galerie Micheline Szwajcer
32 pp., 19 colour photographs
edition of 300

**Some Material Culture Following a Random Method
Based on Aleatory Rules**
Zurich, Mai 36 Galerie
32 pp., 12 colour photographs and 7 black and white photographs
edition of 300

Oeuvre sculpté, travaux pour amateurs
Amsterdam, Roma Publications
112 pp., 49 colour photographs and 31 black and white photographs
edition of 1500 of which 100 copies come as a 'deluxe' paperback
version

2013

A Useless Labour, Apolitical and of Little Moral Significance
Bruxelles, Gevaert Editions
32 pp., coloured letterpress images
edition of 30, signed and numbered

Nouveaux trucs, nouvelles combines
Bruxelles, Gevaert Editions
61 colour slides in a cardboard box with a booklet
edition of 10 + 3 A.P., signed and numbered

2014

This booklet is published as an insert in *Conversation Piece*, initiated by CAHF. It lists the artist's publications in the library of Mu.ZEE – Kunstmuseum aan Zee, Ostend.

Offprint of 100 copies

Typeset in Didot and Franklin Gothic on 130 g Arctic Volume HighWhite
Printed by Stevens Print in Merelbeke (Belgium)
Designed by Koenraad Dedobbeleer in dialogue with Lisa Pommerenke
2013

The image on the back cover of this booklet is taken from Chris Ware's *Acme Novelty Library #07*, published in 1996 by Fantagraphics Books, Seattle.

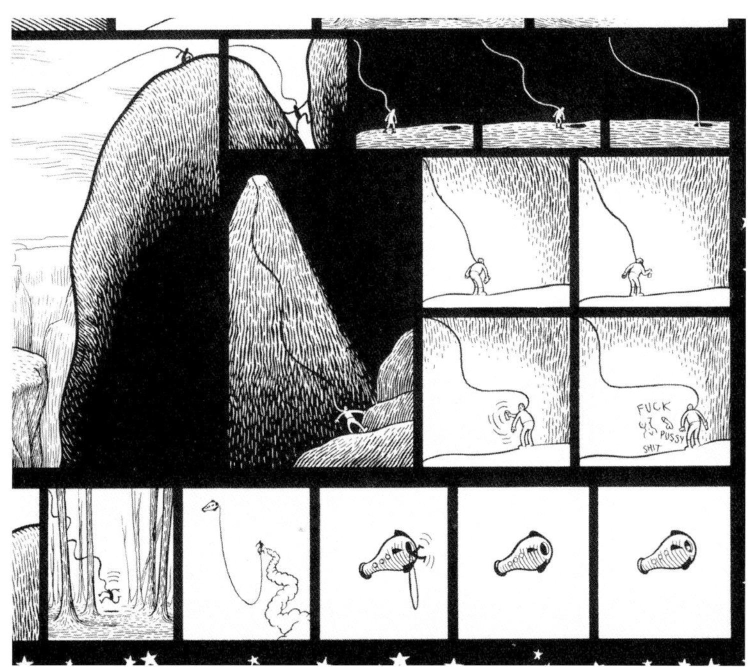

d'un autre auteur

Case Studies

Anne Daems

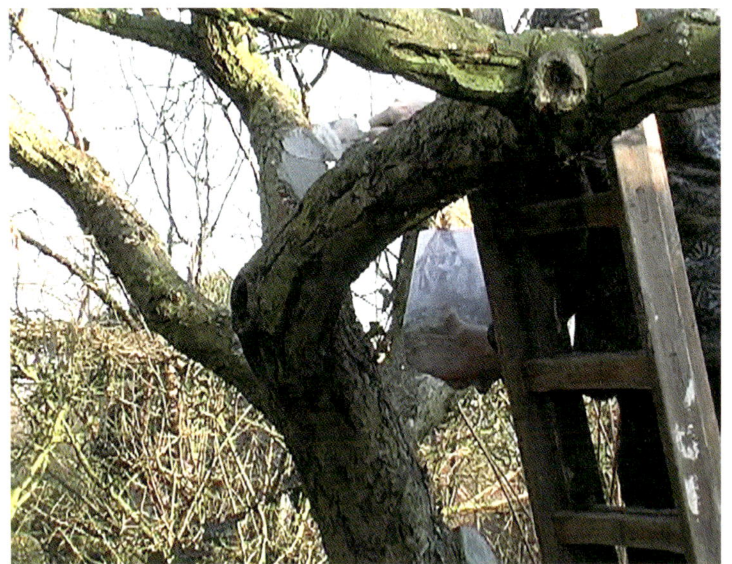

My Father's Garden [video stills], 2008

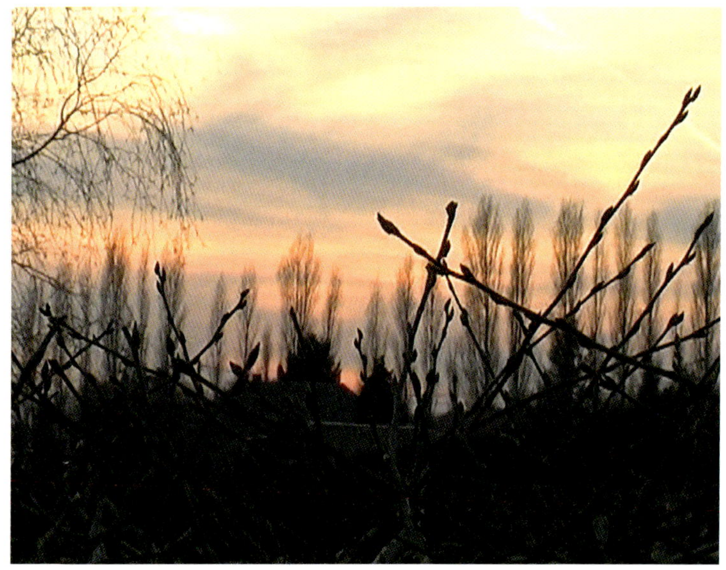

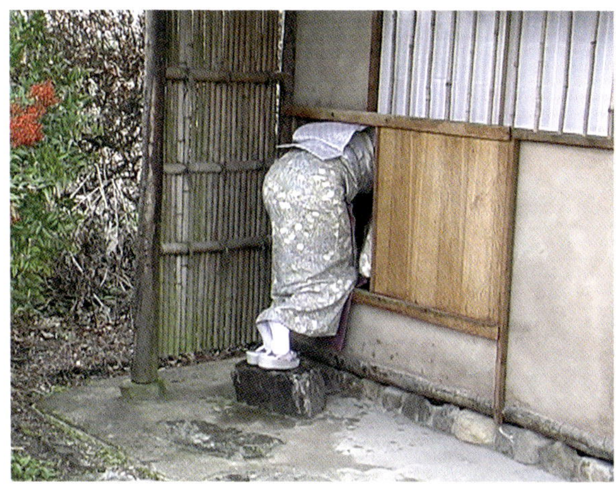

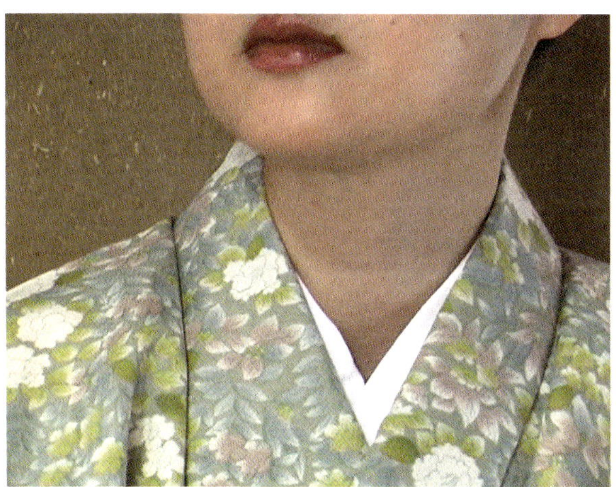

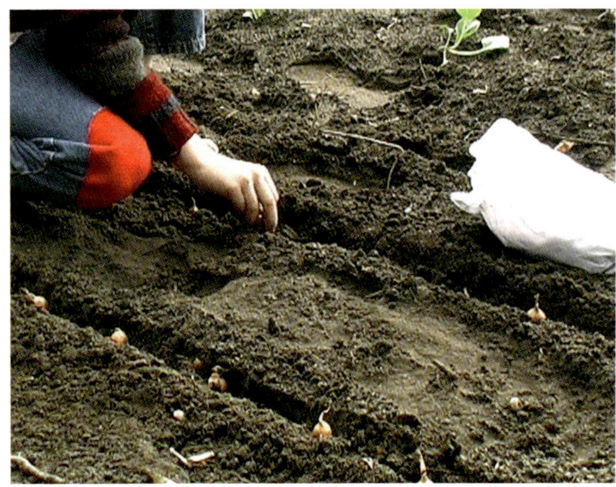

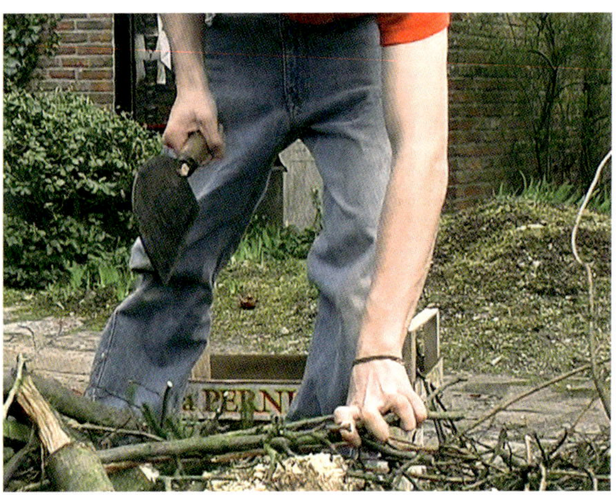

MY FATHER'S GARDEN

When I go visit my father the first thing I do is to go into the garden.
Even in the middle of winter when there is nothing to harvest I put on
some rubber boots, take a big red bowl and scissors and open the
sliding doors. You can always find something: a half frozen red beet,
sprouted turnip leaves, rosemary and rue. With the shovel I dig up
burdock roots. Then I cut off some cherry blossoms and forsythia
branches which start blooming a few days later in a vase in my apart-
ment in Brussels. White, pink, yellow.
When the garden transfers from winter into spring, I like to look at my
father when he turns the moist soil. Sometimes he finds a daikon that
survived winter or a Jerusalem artichoke.
I remember when we were young, after he'd worked in the garden on a
beautiful summer day, he cooked up a delicious and festive supper
with only the weeds he pulled out.
With a saw he cuts off dead branches of an old apple tree and afterwards puts cement in the holes to prevent it from rotting. Cementing is
probably the thing he likes second best after making green tea.
In his garden he has built two Japanese tea pavilions. Although he's
Flemish he practices tea ceremony very seriously and teaches young
Japanese women dressed up in beautiful seasonal kimonos. The
smallest pavilion (2 ¾ tatami) is my favourite. It's based on Teigyokuken,
designed by Kanamori Sowa in the seventeenth century. There is a
little window in the ceiling where the full moon shines through on cloud-
less nights, lighting up the teapot on the charcoal fire or my pillow,
when I stay overnight.
Tomorrow I have to seed clover in my garden.

Anne Daems

The above text originally appeared in *The Loneliness Issue* (2009), the eighth volume of the
magazine *Here and There,* and is reprinted with the artist's and editor's permission.

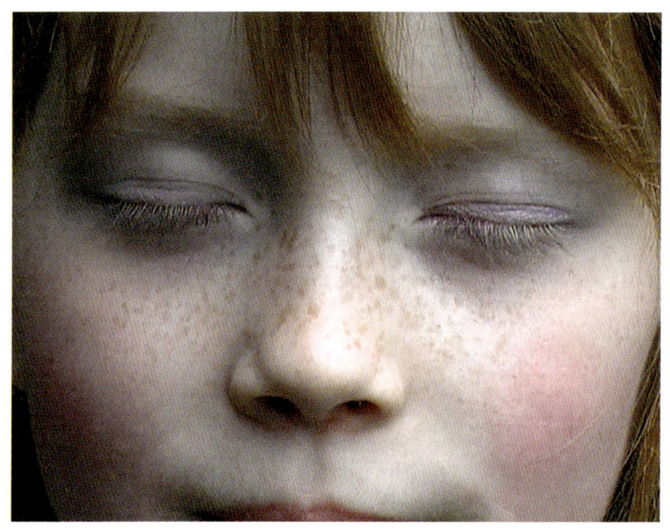

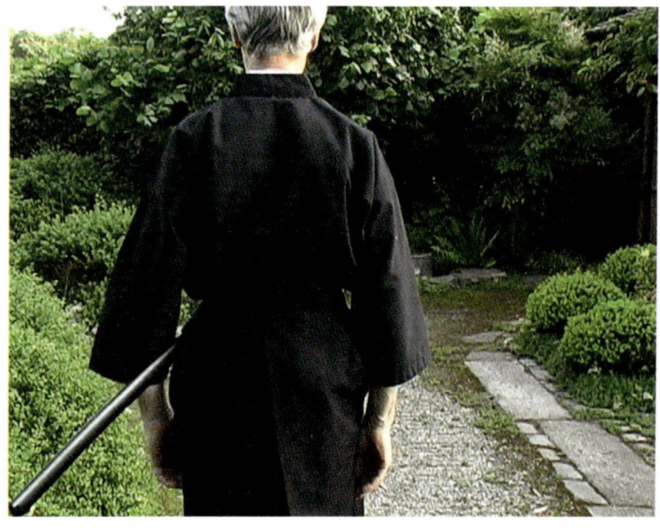

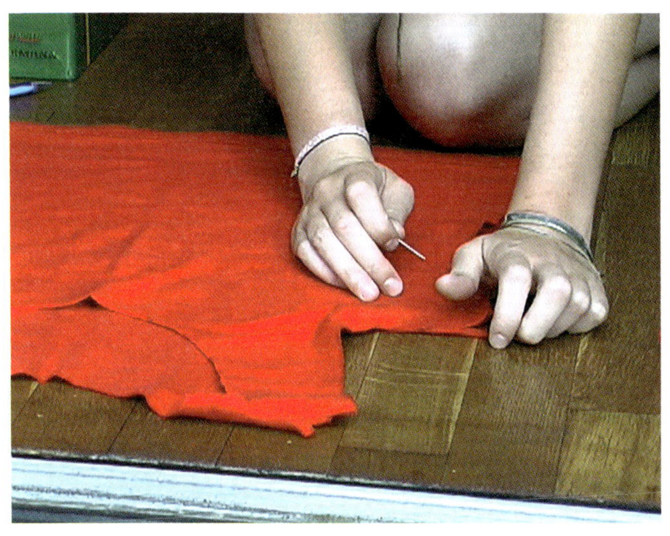

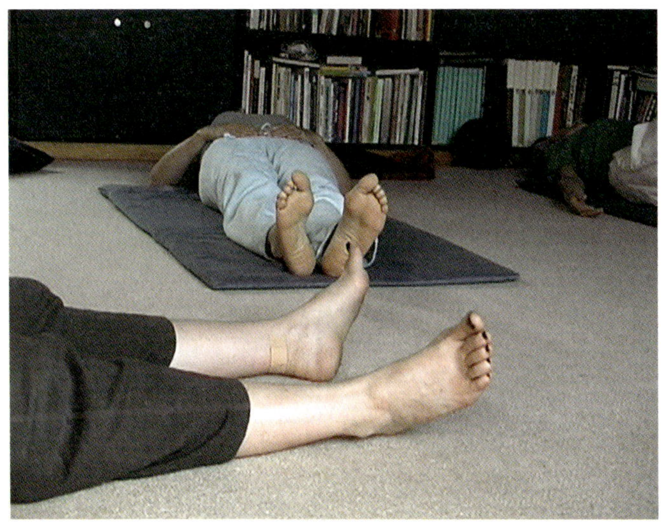

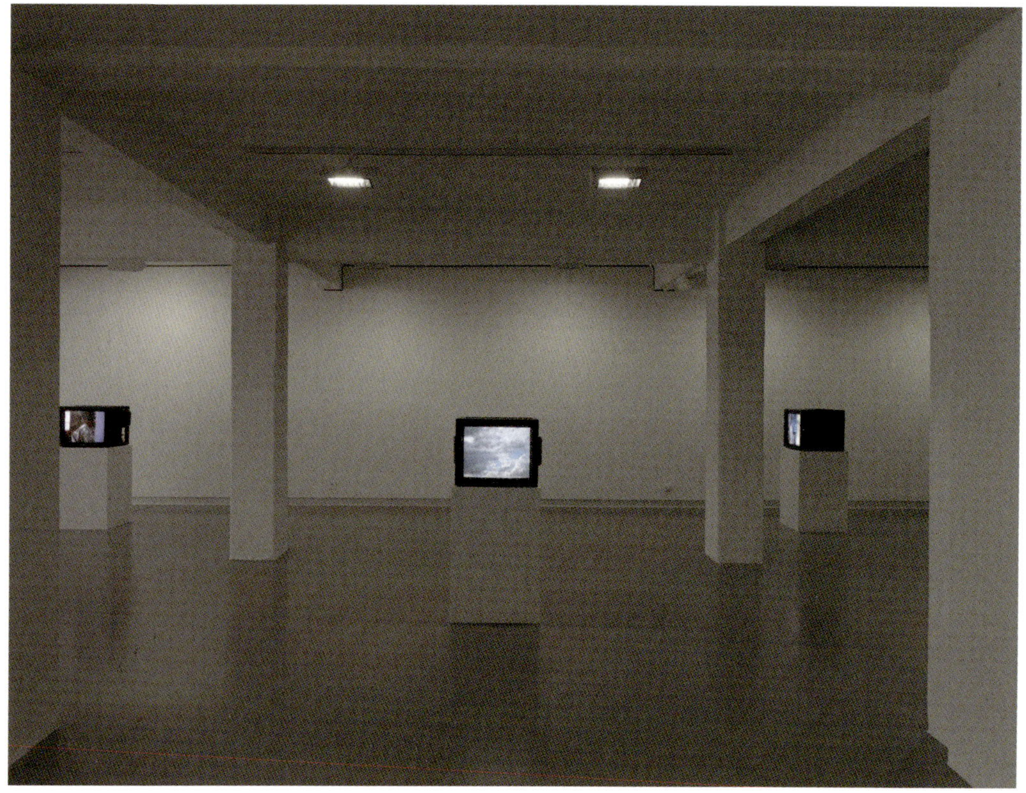

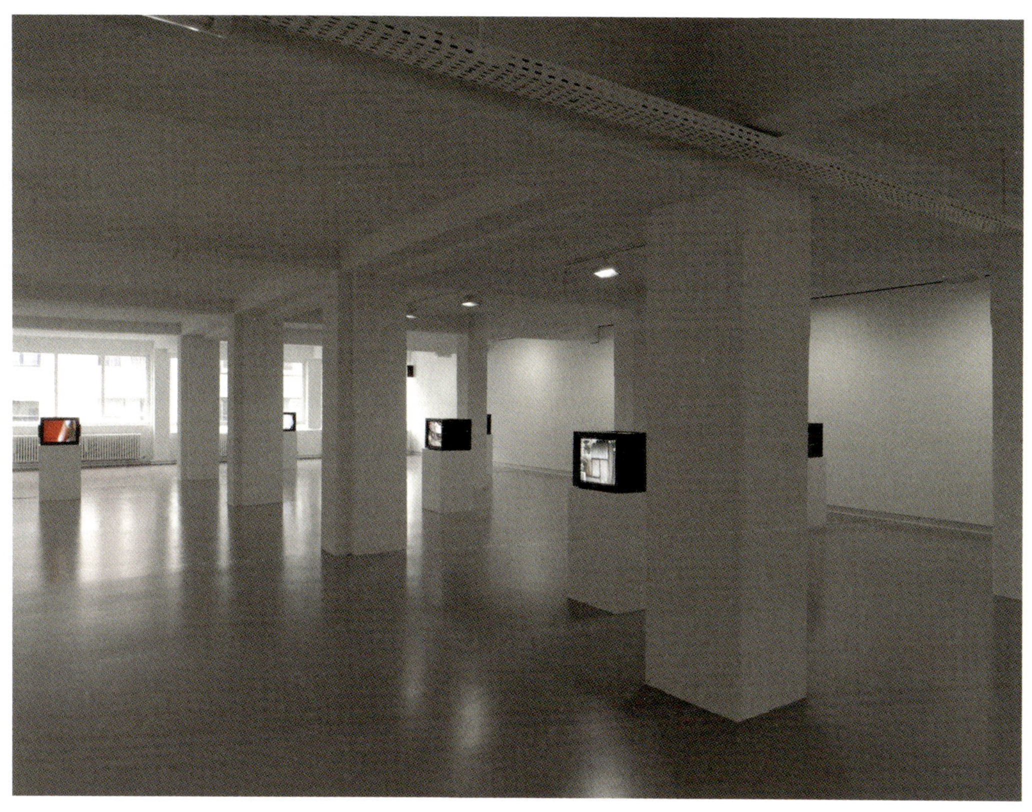

My Father's Garden, 2008
installation views Mu.ZEE

ANNE DAEMS
born in 1966 in Lier, Belgium
lives in Brussels, Belgium

<u>My Father's Garden</u>

2008
six-monitor video installation, dimensions variable, screen ratio 4:3
DVD, colour, stereo audio
video i (two chapters): 9 min. 59 sec.
video ii (one chapter): 7 min. 25 sec.
video iii (two chapters): 11 min. 49 sec.
video iv (one chapter): 5 min. 44 sec.
video v (two chapters): 4 min. 14 sec.
video vi (one chapter): 3 min. 46 sec.
this work is number two from an edition of three plus one artist's proof
inv. no. K002797

Provenance
acquired from Elisa Platteau Galerie, Brussels, in 2010

Exhibited
Bruegel Revisited, National Botanic Garden of Belgium, Meise,
12 May – 3 Sept. 2006 (presented as a single-screen video projection,
differently edited version).
Parsley and Pearls, Nicole Klagsbrun Gallery, New York,
12 June – 15 Aug. 2008 (presented as a single-screen video projection,
differently edited version).
Elke dag, Artis Den Bosch, 's-Hertogenbosch,
7 Sept. – 25 Oct. 2008 (another example exhibited).
Galerie Nadja Vilenne, Liège,
11 Dec. 2008 – 31 March 2009 (another example exhibited).
Galerie Micheline Szwajcer, Antwerp,
19 March – 2 May 2009 (another example exhibited).
Let's Pick the Cherries First, Elisa Platteau Galerie, Brussels,
2 July – 19 Sept. 2009 (presented as a double-monitor video installation,
another example exhibited).
Het zelfportret, het huis en de seizoenen, Mu.ZEE, Ostend,
17 Sept. 2011 – 15 Jan. 2012.

Literature
Hilde Van Gelder, ed., *Bruegel Revisited,* exh. cat., Stichting Kunstboek,
Oostkamp, 2006 (illustrated in colour).
Anne Daems, 'My Father's Garden', in: Nakako Hayashi, ed.,
Here and There, vol. 8: *The Loneliness Issue,* Nieves, Zurich, 2008,
pp. 28 – 29 (illustrated in colour).

Valérie Mannaerts

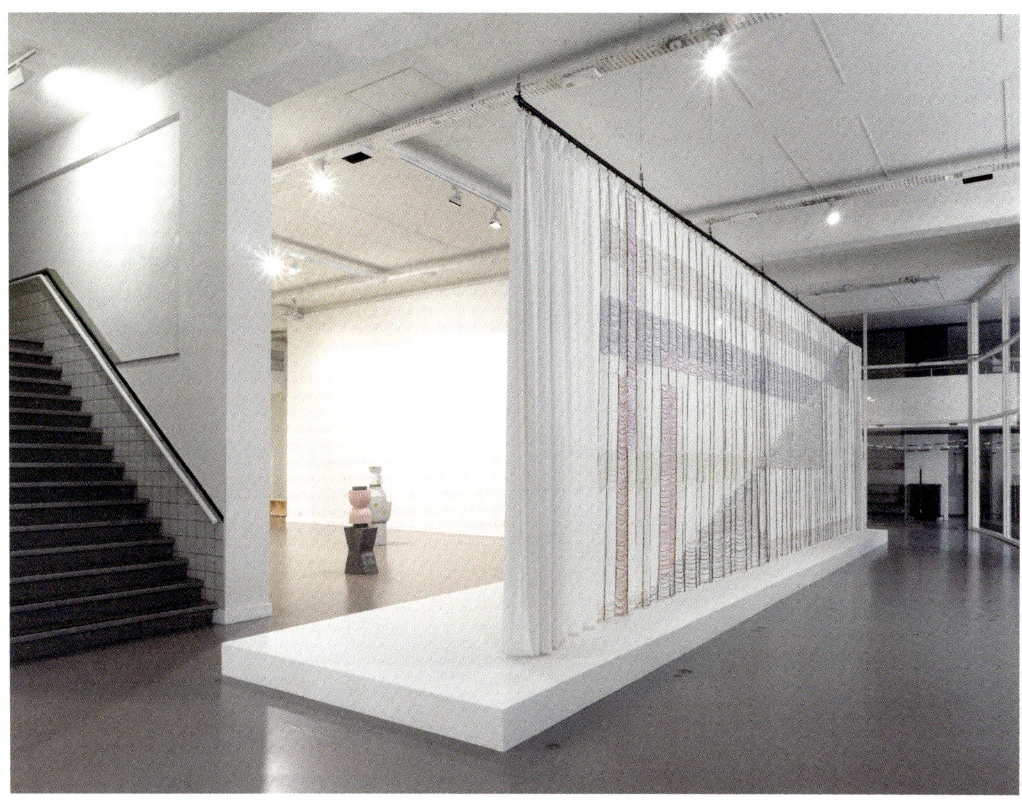

Blood Flow (curtain), 2010
installation view Mu.ZEE

VALÉRIE MANNAERTS IN CONVERSATION WITH
BJÖRN SCHERLIPPENS ON THE WORKS RECENTLY
ACQUIRED BY Mu.ZEE

Björn Scherlippens: In 2009 Phillip Van den Bossche invited you to participate in the third edition of *Beaufort,* the triennial of contemporary art held along the Belgian coastline. You created a new work for that occasion, *If travel is searching and home what's been found,* an ensemble of nine massive concrete sculptures that was installed on the beach of Oostduinkerke. To what extent did the spatial context—the public space, the beach, the sea—play a role in the development of the concept?

Valérie Mannaerts: A huge amount of information converges in a location such as the beach of Oostduinkerke, with a vast array of visual stimuli present in the landscape. I wanted to create a work that would integrate in the setting without however compromising its autonomy. After my first visit to the site, I felt the need to mark off a few points that would emphasize and define the site. I wanted to introduce new forms of signage with a proper logic and meaning, whose presence is not geared toward spectacle but is rather absorbed in the dynamics of the place.

The sculptures were cast in concrete. Was this a logical choice from the outset?

There are already many elements in concrete on the beach and it seemed obvious to me to elaborate my concept in this material. The organizers of *Beaufort* had also pointed out the rough environment, and the duration of the exhibition. Concrete was a natural choice, a material commonly used on the Belgian coast and sufficiently resistant. However, I wanted to affect the massive character of concrete. During that period, I visited a number of houses and buildings by Le Corbusier, an architect who dealt with this material in a very sculptural way. What influenced me was his use of colour and the strong wood structure he left visible in the concrete. This grain structure made me realize that concrete is a liquid material that acquires a fixed form when it hardens in a formwork. I had never considered the negative-positive formwork system before; quite a different way of thinking about architecture.

Architecture is in this way approached in a much more sculptural manner.
I love the idea of the mould leaving traces in the new material, that the

veins and seams of the wood remain visible. The material acquires a very organic feel. Today, concrete can be poured to a smooth finish, but in Le Corbusier's time this was not the case. I suspect that he deliberately emphasized this technical aspect.

You have created a total of nine concrete sculptures. How did you choose and sculpt the various forms?
I had created five basic shapes from which I could choose to assemble the totems, and this would relate them formally to one another, even if each work is different. I was concerned with identity and variation within a given group, in this specific location. Another important element is the use of the colour planes that greatly define the sculptures and give the concrete—a material that is naturally hard and solid—a playful character. This contradiction is what also appealed to me in the colour usage of Le Corbusier. Through a simple intervention, he could affect the character of a material. I chose a number of colours from the palette he conceived specifically for concrete. I chose colours that would suit the beach, refer to ice cream and beach towels…

How did tourists react to the totems?
People did not hesitate to approach the artworks. Some sculptures were used by children for pretend horse riding, or as a platform for shooting bottles or as a towel rail… The fact that I had grouped the works turned them into a kind of feature or marker. People seemed to like to be in the vicinity of the sculptures with their beach chairs. Just as they seek shelter in the dunes to be protected from the wind, they sought shelter and cosiness near my work, which acted as an anchor point in a vast, expansive area.

Was this the kind of interaction you had hoped for or expected?
I was happy that the sculptures functioned in this way. Some friends told me afterwards that the work was very inviting to the touch, despite the fact that it was made of concrete. The totems do not seem to be very heavy, but they are. These are miniature monuments that entirely overturn the imposing character of a concrete sculpture. The feeling of massiveness is countered by the playful shapes and colours. I have been told that people like to be in the vicinity of the work, and I do consider that as a compliment.

I was very curious to see if the work would also function in a museum context, a place where the viewer's behaviour is strongly conditioned and artworks are rarely touched. After six months at the beach, the sculptures looked visibly worn, the ensemble coated with a patina that remained visible even in the context of the museum. This, to me, only strengthened their autonomy.

In 2010 you had two solo exhibitions: *Blood Flow* in Antwerp and *Diamond Dancer* in Amsterdam. All the works you presented there were explicitly named after the exhibition. It makes me wonder: can those works function autonomously or do they form part of a cluster?
For me, a title functions as a chapter in my work that covers a period. Every work is autonomous but it bears a main title as a reference to that period and that group of works. It is comparable to the title of an album that groups a number of songs. The singles can have an independent existence but they are placed in relation to other songs. I build an exhibition in this manner and sometimes there are some works taken out because they no longer fit within the whole or vice versa. I love the internal logic of such a group.

One of the largest works in *Blood Flow* was *Blood Flow (curtain),* a more than eighteen-meter long floor-to-ceiling curtain that divides the space like a giant partition. This work was purchased by Phillip Van den Bossche for Mu.ZEE. What fascinated him was how, with this work, you explored the intersection between applied art, design and art. Craftsmanship obviously plays a role in this work. How long did you work on the curtain?
The production itself took two weeks. Because of its huge size, I worked on it with an assistant. I translated the sketch of the design by means of a numbered grid onto the curtain. I wanted to make that methodology visible. The creative process itself appealed to me, not in the least because the needle and thread brought me very close to the 1:1 scale again. I love the contradiction between the enormous scale of the work and the lightness of the material. You fold it up and it transforms into two small-sized volumes. At Extra City, I placed a number of small bronze

sculptures opposite the work. Painting them in marble and wood patterns dissimulated the expected monumentality which gave the sculptures another identity. In *The Self-portrait, the House and the Seasons* (2011), a group show with reflections on the work of Jean Brusselmans, I placed the curtain opposite the concrete totems of *If travel is searching and home what's been found.* In both setups I have upturned the expectations the material conjures up, creating a tension or a form of surprise I often consciously seek out.

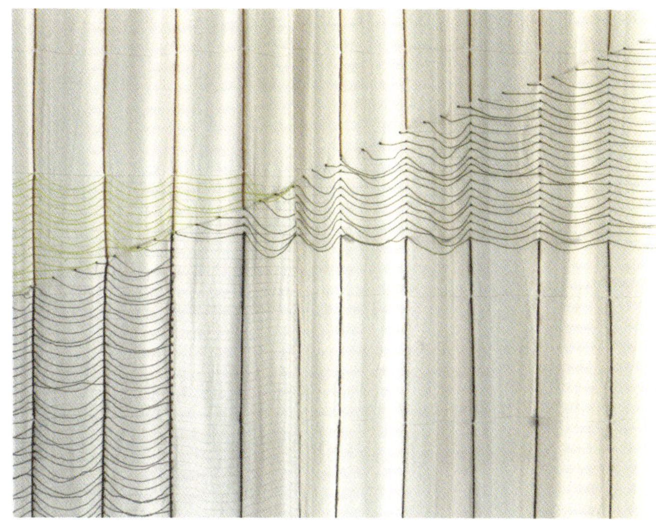

Blood Flow (curtain) [detail], 2010

The curtain was not simply hung in the exhibition space. You put it on a gigantic white base which gives the work a sculptural character.
I did not only want to hang the work like a two-dimensional curtain, but clearly also wanted it to function as a sculptural and architectural intervention. The base emphasizes the object and determines the way it is perceived. The extra space I made to the rear of the pedestal plays an important role in the perception, the use and definition of the space.

In Amsterdam you exhibited *Diamond Dancer (paravent),* a wooden folding screen with drawings fitted to its front side, standing on a pedestal with a showcase. What do the drawings on the folding screen refer to?
The drawings represent an imaginary atelier. You see objects that are present in my studio and also a number of fictional elements that together create an image of an artist's studio. The drawings represent the utensils an artist needs to make his work, such as brushes or a vase of flowers, but also shells and stones, organic shapes that can stimulate the imagination. The whole setting of the work rather acts as a projection of a mental space. One of the references I was using was a studiolo I had

visited in the Ducal Palace of Urbino. The study room is worked out in marquetry and presents walls with books, foreign objects, work materials, windows… It is an intimate space for reflection, study and imagination.

Throughout history, a folding screen has always been a carrier of images. It is also an archetypal object in the studio of an artist, just like a wood-burning stove, for example. At the same time, it is an object that hovers on the boundary between two- and three-dimensionality, a quality that greatly interests me. A folding screen is both image and object. You can shift between these two dimensions through simple manipulation, creating a flexible space and object.

Just like the curtain, the folding screen is a spatial element that creates a certain separation which the viewer can walk around. What role does the glass case have in this?
The curtain and the folding screen are two elements that conceal or hide something. They are objects that stimulate a certain feeling of expecta-tion or anticipation in the viewer. The nature of these objects makes that the imagination and projection of the viewer is absorbed into the work. The placement of the glass in front of the object, as it were, doubles the frame of projection. It also becomes a screen in which the viewer is reflected. In this sense, *Diamond Dancer (paravent)* focuses on the acts of looking and showing, and imagination.

Both works have a theatrical dimension.
That's right. These are objects that are evidently displayed and placed on a pedestal. Both the curtain and the folding screen are archetypal elements in the performing arts. Theatricality in this sense forms part of these works' identity.

To the extent where the presentation itself becomes the subject…
In retrospect, it seems as if both works in the exhibitions in Antwerp and Amsterdam acted as each other's counterpart. They have a similar presence and function, and have a clear composition. I think it is fantas-tic that both works have been brought together in the Mu.ZEE.

In 2011, Mu.ZEE organized the *March on Ostend* in the frame of *P.P.P. – Public Private Paintings,* and made a call to artists for a flag design. You

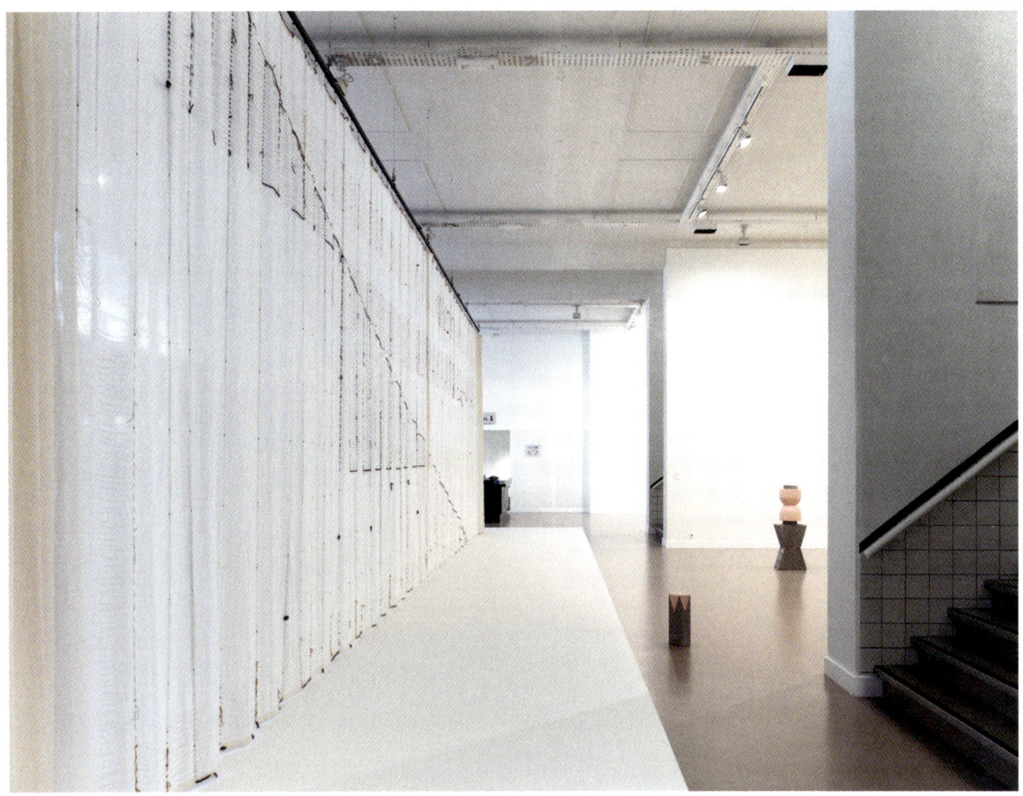

Before starting on the big curtain, I had made a test version with different types of wool and colours. When I was asked to design a flag,
I worked out that test version. The title lends the flag a formal character
through which I also wanted to express its status. It is a study, a play
with composition and colour. I donated *Geometrical Fantasy* to Mu.ZEE
precisely because of its strong link with *Blood Flow (curtain).*

Ostend, 20 January 2012

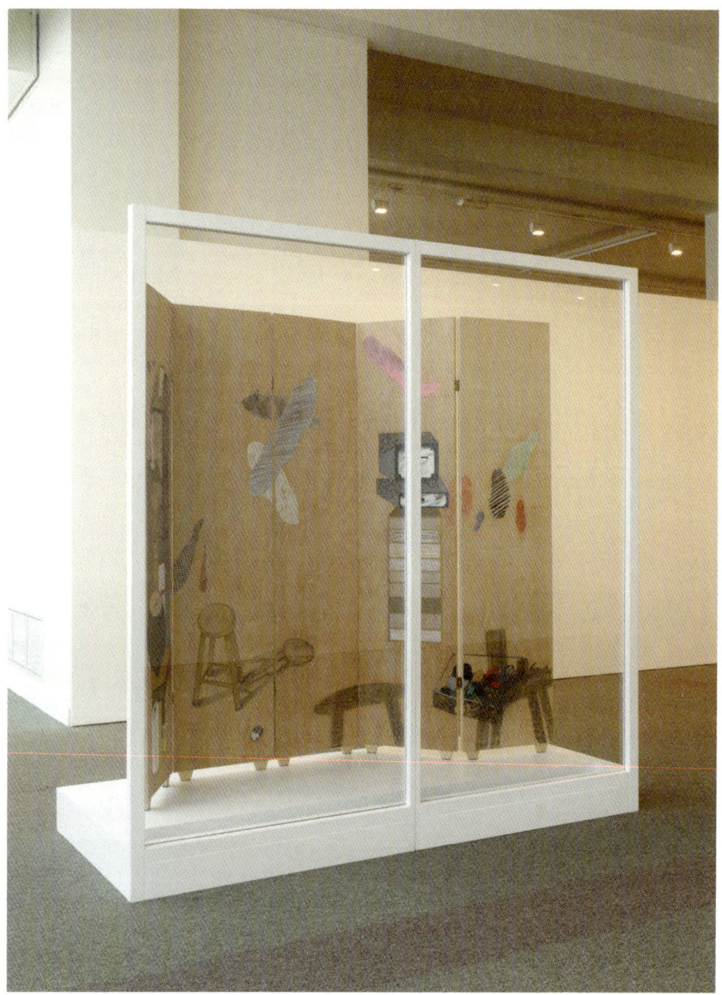

Diamond Dancer (paravent), 2010

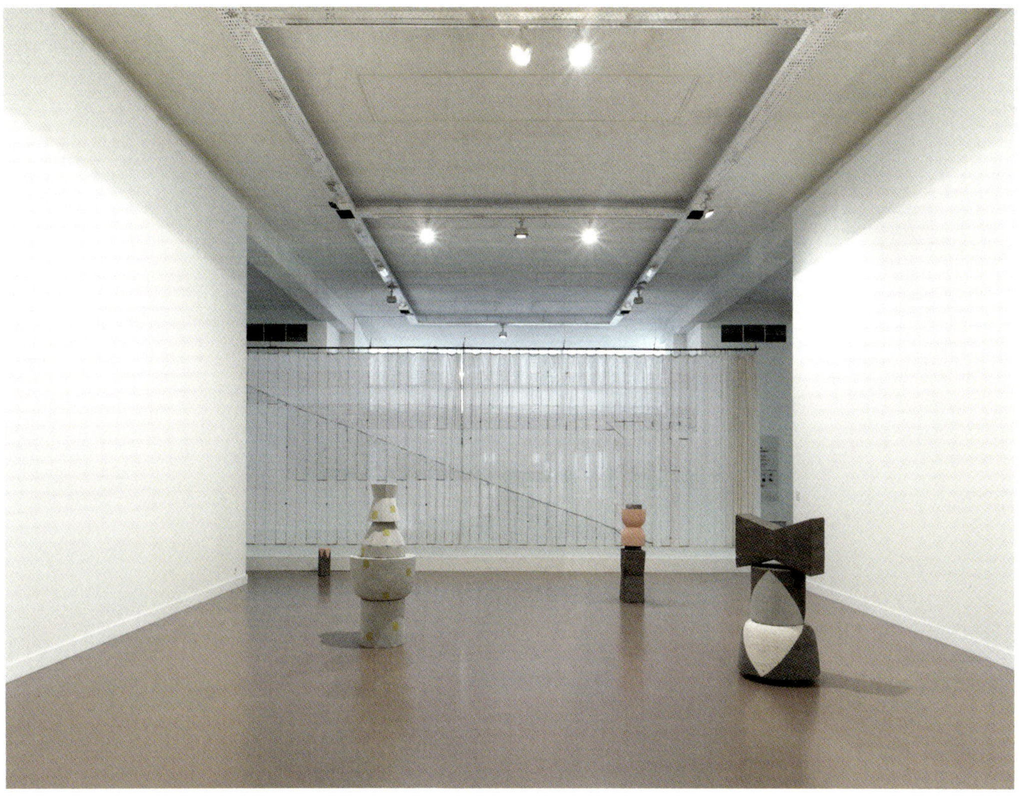

If travel is searching and home what's been found, 2009

VALÉRIE MANNAERTS
born in 1974 in Brussels, Belgium
lives in Brussels, Belgium

Blood Flow (curtain)
2010
graphite and wool embroidery on cotton;
painted wooden pedestal, rollers, rail, metal hooks
380 × 1250 × 244 cm
inv. no. MZ000005

Provenance
acquired directly from the artist in 2010

Exhibited
Blood Flow, Extra City, Kunsthal Antwerpen,
Antwerp, 21 May – 11 July 2010.
Het zelfportret, het huis en de seizoenen, Mu.ZEE,
Ostend, 17 Sept. 2011 – 15 Jan. 2012.

Literature
An exhibition – another exhibition, exh. cat., Sternberg
Press, Berlin / New York, 2011 (illustrated in colour).

Diamond Dancer (paravent)
2010
showcase with pedestal in painted wood and glass;
wooden screen with drawings in oil pastel, pastel
and pencil
240 × 240 × 105 cm
inv. no. MZ000076

Provenance
acquired from Elisa Platteau & Cie Galerie, Brussels,
in 2011

Exhibited
Diamond Dancer, de Appel arts centre, Amsterdam,
17 Dec. 2010 – 27 Feb. 2011.
Elisa Platteau & Cie Galerie, Brussels,
15 April – 21 May 2011.
Het zelfportret, het huis en de seizoenen, Mu.ZEE,
Ostend, 17 Sept. 2011 – 15 Jan. 2012.

Literature
An exhibition – another exhibition, exh. cat., Sternberg
Press, Berlin / New York, 2011 (illustrated in colour).

Geometrical Fantasy
2010
pencil, wool embroidery and nine metal rings on cotton
187.5 × 262 cm
inv. no. MZ000077

Provenance
gift from the artist in 2011

Exhibited
Mars op Oostende, various public locations in Ostend,
9 Nov. 2010.
P.P.P. – Public Private Paintings, Mu.ZEE, Ostend,
9 Oct. 2010 – 9 Jan. 2011.

Literature
Vlaggenboek Mu.ZEE / Mars op Oostende, Mu.ZEE,
Ostend, 2011 (illustrated in colour).

**If travel is searching and home what's been found
(yellow dots)**
2009
concrete, silicate paint in Le Corbusier colours
140 × 60 × 60 cm
**If travel is searching and home what's been found
(bow tie with pink body)**
2009
concrete, silicate paint in Le Corbusier colours
118 × 60 × 60 cm
**If travel is searching and home what's been found
(pink bow tie)**
2009
concrete, silicate paint in Le Corbusier colours
115 × 40 × 30 cm
If travel is searching and home what's been found (napkin)
2009
concrete, silicate paint in Le Corbusier colours
40 × 20 × 20 cm
inv. no. K002791

Provenance
gift from the artist in 2009

Exhibited
Beaufort03, various public locations along the Belgian
coastline, 28 March – 4 Oct. 2010 (presented as a nine-part
sculptural installation at the beach in Oostduinkerke).
Het zelfportret, het huis en de seizoenen, Mu.ZEE, Ostend,
17 Sept. 2011 – 15 Jan. 2012.

Literature
Beaufort03, exh. cat., Borgerhoff & Lamberigts, Ghent,
2009 (illustrated in colour).

Sven Augustijnen

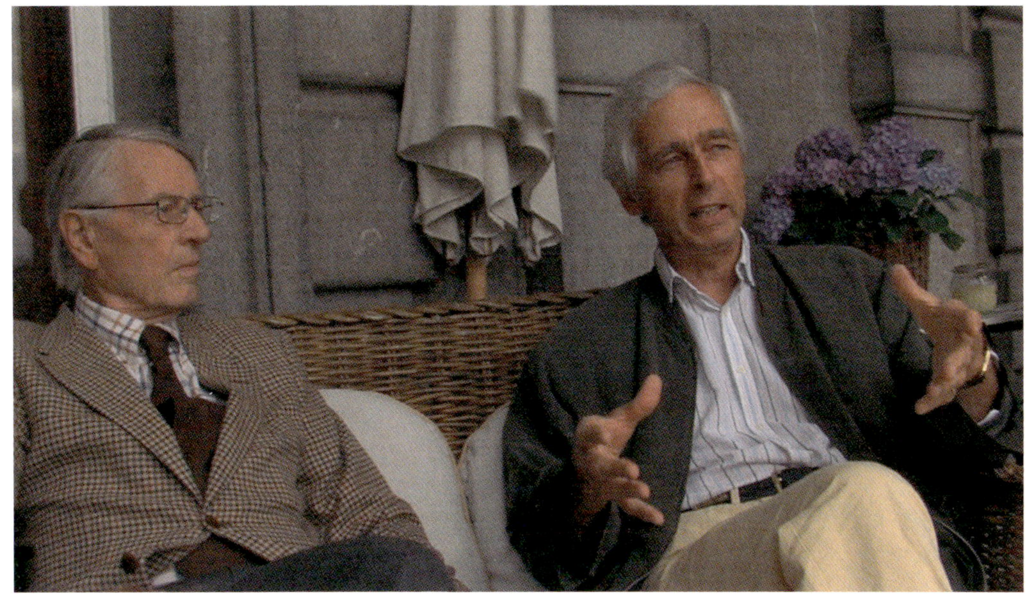

Spectres [video stills], 2011

SVEN AUGUSTIJNEN IN CONVERSATION WITH BJÖRN SCHERLIPPENS

Fifty years after his assassination, Patrice Lumumba, Prime Minister of the newly independent Congo, is back to haunt Belgium. Through commemorations, encounters and a return visit, a top-ranking Belgian civil servant who was in Elisabethville on that tragic day of 17 January 1961 attempts to exorcise the ghosts of the past. To the sound of St John Passion by J.S. Bach, *Spectres* plunges us into one of the blackest days of the Belgian Congo's decolonisation. An examination of the biopolitical body, this feature-length film by Sven Augustijnen exposes the fine line separating legitimation and historiography and the traumatic question of responsibility and debt. (source: www.augusteorts.be)

Mu.ZEE co-financed Augustijnen's *Spectres* project which today has become, just like his *L'Histoire Belge* (2007), part of the collection. This interview focuses on the years of research that preceded the film, in which a tangle of major and minor issues became intertwined to form a complex historical web, only to conclude that the ghosts of the past are much more part of this story than is initially assumed. Even today, the brutal murder of Patrice Lumumba remains a hot topic of international attention. In December 2012, at the request of the relatives of the victim, the Brussels Chamber of Indictment gave the federal prosecution green light to initiate a judicial inquiry into the murder. In June of 2011, just a few weeks after the premiere of *Spectres,* the family members of the former prime minister filed a complaint against a dozen Belgians, including Jacques Brassinne de La Buissière, the central character in Augustijnen's film. The family accuses him and nine others of being involved in the murder.

Björn Scherlippens: *Spectres* premiered in May 2011 at the Kunsten-festivaldesarts in Brussels. It was quite a long time in the making. When did you actually start thinking about the film?

Sven Augustijnen: The idea originated in 2005. At the time I had published an article in the newspaper *De Tijd* (12 October 2005), in the context of the exhibition *Information / Transformation* in Extra City. In it, I historically situated the European institutions in the Brussels Leopold district. The original plans for that district had been initiated under Leopold I, but it was mainly Leopold II—the builder king—who elaborated and developed the Royal Route (Cinquantenaire, Royal Palace, Palace of Justice, Botanique, etc.). *Panorama* includes an interview with Etienne Davignon. As Vice President of the European Commission, he played an

important role in the late seventies in the contest between Brussels and
Strasbourg for the building of an International Congress Centre to
the size and needs of the European Parliament. What is important in the
context of *Spectres,* however, is the fact that he, as a governmental
employee of the Minister of Foreign Affairs, Pierre Wigny, played a major
role in the Lumumba affair in 1960. The *Panorama* article does not
investigate his murder in depth, but does touch upon the subject.

With *Cher Pourquoi Pas?* (2007), a special issue of the art magazine
A Prior, your attention strongly shifted to Lumumba. What was your
approach for this article?
Cher Pourquoi Pas? functions as a magazine in a magazine. I especially
wanted to focus on the involvement of Pierre Davister in the kidnap-
ping of Tshombe on 30 June 1967. Davister was a French journalist for
the weekly *Pourquoi Pas?* and the editor of *Spécial.* Moïse Tshombe
was kidnapped during a plane hijacking and brought to Algeria, where
he spent two years under house arrest and finally died under mysterious
circumstances. Tshombe obviously played an important role in the
Lumumba affair. In *Spectres* I visit Tshombe's tomb in the cemetery of
Etterbeek with his relatives.

In 2008, you realised the photographic work *Les Demoiselles de
Bruxelles.* We are shown a statue of Leopold II together with an image
of an African prostitute. A plaque in the Rue d'Orléans indicates
where Karl Marx lived from 1846 to 1848, but we are mainly shown a lot
of architectural and sculptural remains of the Brussels colonial past.
Les Demoiselles very explicitly links the spectres of Leopold II and Karl
Marx to the prostitution district around the Avenue Louise in Brussels
and conjures up, in this sense, quite a number of connotations. Marx
and Friedrich Engels wrote the Communist Manifesto together in Brussels.
Its publication in 1848 had a revolutionary impact on the European
politics. Leopold I expelled Marx and Engels from the country because
of the political turmoil. The revolutions of 1848 very much affected
the Belgian royal family. Queen Marie-Louise of Orléans — whom the
Avenue Louise was later named after — had to stand idly by as her family
was expelled from France. This must have been quite traumatising for
the children of the royal couple as well, not only for Leopold II, but also
for his sister Charlotte, the Empress of Mexico.

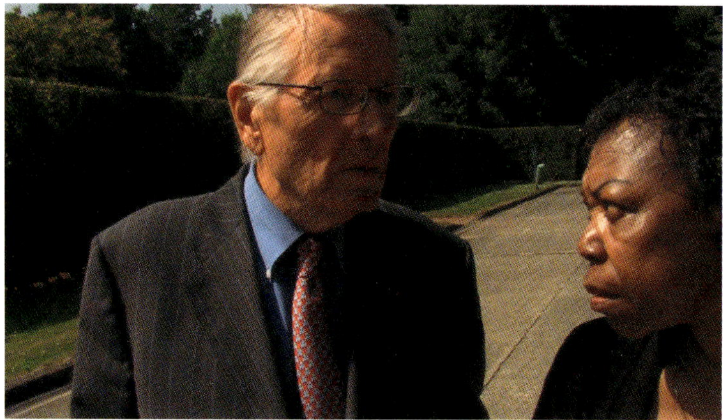

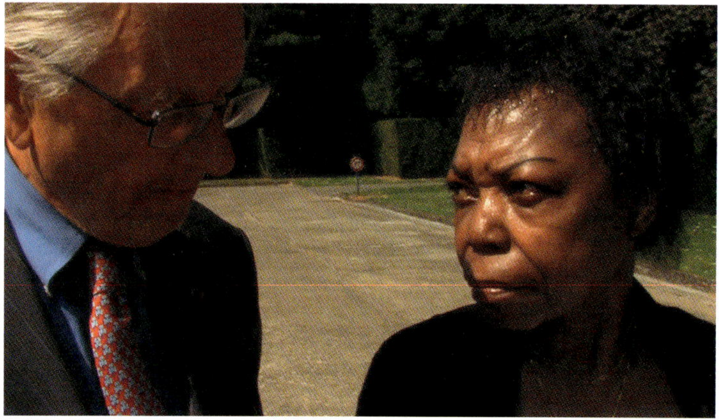

In *L'Histoire Belge* (2007), you collected a series of photos that present an overview of the royal history of Belgium. You approach the issue in a much broader sense and place the Congo story in a wider context. This story is included as one of the many elements in the history of our country.

The projects discussed above, all originated in the investigation and finally lead to *Spectres.* These are secondary story lines that function autonomously but also fit into the context. *L'Histoire Belge* followed in the slipstream of these projects and created possibilities for me to interconnect a number of fragments in Belgian history. It is for example very interesting to situate the tragic history of Charlotte in a wider political and familial context. In *Spectres,* I initially wanted to turn my attention to three main characters that haunt our history like ghosts:

King Leopold II, Patrice Lumumba and Karl Marx. In the end, I chose to mainly focus on the figure of Lumumba; the presence of the two other spectres remains more veiled.

Jacques Brassinne is just one of the key witnesses in the Lumumba story, but many of the other persons involved are no longer alive today. This automatically created a certain focus on his personage, and by extension *Spectres* became, in a way, a film about the relatives, the family of those involved. Brassinne was very much intent on retracing the trip to Katanga. He wanted to find the tree Lumumba was shot against. In 1988, he managed to locate the tree and now he wanted to show off his find like a proud hunter. It soon became clear that the storyline surrounding his figure had a strong structure with a clear beginning and ending. I had set up several story lines but some of them were not strong enough to stand alongside the dramatically complex story of Brassinne. I am thinking of a recording made in Ostend, showing a memorial held in memory of the murder of Lumumba on 17 January 2010. There was a procession with a marching band through the city with stops at the monuments of the colonial past. Fifty roses were thrown into the sea from the pier, as a final tribute. This made for some beautiful images but the fragment did not fit in the final scenario.

In 2009, on the occasion of the upcoming fiftieth anniversary of independence of Congo, the newspaper *Le Soir* published a series of opinion pieces in the section *Cartes blanches.* In the first opinion piece (*Le Soir*, 28 January 2009), the *Collectif Mémoires Coloniales* pointed to the Belgian responsibility and specifically referred to a telex from Harold d'Aspremont Lynden. The collective followed Ludo De Witte's interpretation of the facts. Arnaud d'Aspremont Lynden firmly refuted his father's involvement in a second opinion piece (*Le Soir*, 11 February 2009). I had been in contact with Brassinne before that but the renewed interest in the controversy also marked a new start for the project. I asked him if he wanted to present his story together with d'Aspremont Lynden in front of the camera.

Ludo De Witte's absence in *Spectres* is remarkable.
When I first contacted Brassinne about my project in 2006, he replied: 'Ludo De Witte is my spectre.'

Which witnesses did you have on your wish list at the outset? We are talking about events that took place more than fifty years ago.
I very much wanted to visit Larry Devlin, the active CIA operative in Congo in 1960, who played a very crucial role in the diplomatic intervention of the United States in the country's struggle for independence. He died in late 2008. He represented the spectre of communism that I wanted to explicitly integrate.

You talk about 'spectres', and not about 'ghosts' or 'phantoms', which allows you to consciously introduce an entire philosophical context. Was the choice of this title a device to add layers of content to the film, and if so, to what extent?
The years of research involved an intense study of all the literature, which was not only limited to the history of Congo. As I have indicated before in the context of *Les Demoiselles de Bruxelles,* I have intensively studied the episode of Karl Marx in Brussels. The Communist Manifesto literally begins by stating that 'the spectre of Communism haunts Europe.' The various neo-Marxist discourses are interesting study topics as well. After the fall of the Berlin Wall in 1989, Jacques Derrida wrote *Spectres de Marx* (1993). I have weaved a complex web of various threads of information that was subsequently distilled, directly or indirectly, into a scenario. The final scenario was reduced to one main character who sets in search of a number of other figures, but in the end all that

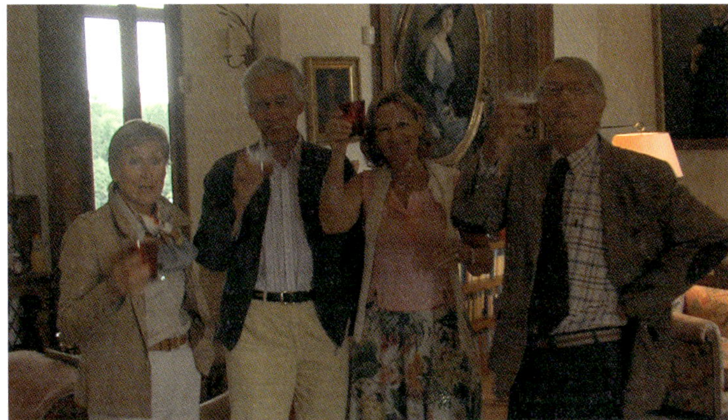

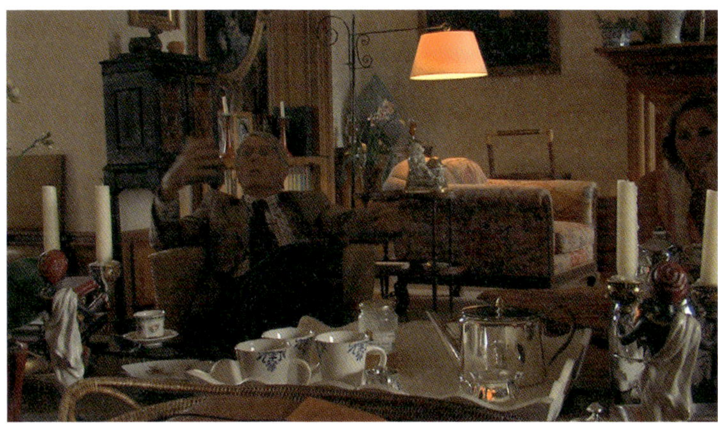

research, no matter how far it reached, ultimately led to one particular synthesis: there are ghosts that should be expelled, pursued and exorcised. Those involved try to come to terms with the past, try to suppress or sublimate it, for example. I, as the brain behind the film, am part of it as well. For I enter into an intimate relationship with the research and the (main) character.

Of course there are images of the speeches of King Boudewijn and Lumumba at the proclamation of Congo's independence, but this material is—even though we are talking about more than fifty years ago— still very current. It is almost 'live' material, haunted as it is by so many

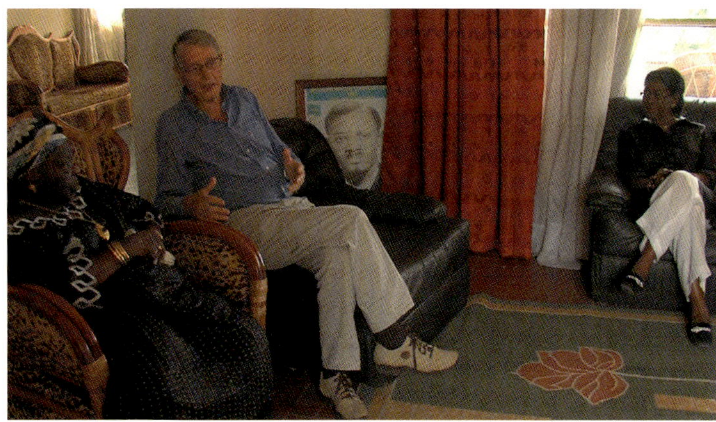

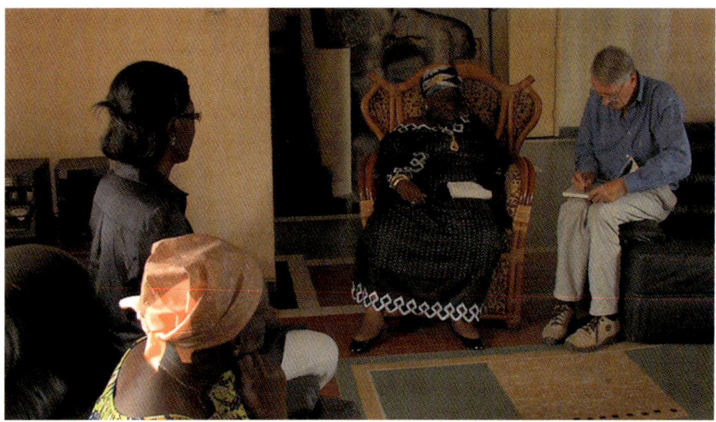

ghosts. *Spectres* deals with very specific historical issues but depicts the 'now', the experience of this history and the way in which it haunts us.

You consciously show Lumumba only once, and even then the fragment is very 'uncomfortable', as it follows Brassinne visiting Pauline, the wife of Lumumba, and her children in Kinshasa. His portrait stands in a corner of the living room; it becomes an unavoidable image in the shot during the difficult conversation between Brassinne and Pauline.

They talk about the last picture that was taken of him, when he was imprisoned in early December 1960. I thought it was interesting to show the daughter's expression of horror as she imagines the photograph rather than the picture itself. Apart from that, there are no photos of the murder of Lumumba. Everything was made to disappear. His body was destroyed and there is nothing left but the rumours that two gold teeth remain in Gerard Soete's possession. Some argue that they were thrown in the North Sea, hence the memorial in Ostend, of which I spoke earlier. I felt it was more interesting to evoke images rather than to explicitly show them.

Johann Sebastian Bach's St John Passion, used throughout Spectres, makes for a remarkable soundtrack. The music creates a tremendous feeling of tension.
The *St John Passion* is the most anti-Semitic of the four gospels and I have used it as a way to refer to the telex of 14 January 1961 sent by Colonel Marlière from Leopoldville, in which he requested authorisation to transfer Lumumba to Elizabethville: 'Request the Jew's approval to receive Satan.' Tshombe was the Jew — the traitor, the man with the money — and Lumumba was Satan — vilified as a communist. The structure of the narratives of the assassin and the person to be eliminated, as well as the person who orchestrates everything and the one who washes his hands in innocence, is contained in that one sentence.

Brassinne turned the Lumumba murder investigation into his life's work, but you, as a 'maker', have conducted your own research as well. When I was watching the film, I wondered who was the actual author. Who plays the lead role? You or Brassinne?
Someone pointed out to me that there is a double involved. It did not take me thirty years, but there is a parallel between the unfinished past that keeps haunting Brassinne and a project like *Spectres.* In one way or another, this project is not yet completed. We have come a long way. Also, it was a quite an ordeal financially to realise the project, but aside from that, *Spectres* remains open-ended and closes with the announcement that the widow and sons of Lumumba have undertaken litigation against a dozen surviving Belgians who were involved in the affair, including, apparently, Jacques Brassinne. But the — very understandable — question remains: Who is the artist? Who is the historian?

Brussels, 11 November 2011

Edited with additions by Mieke Mels in dialogue with Sven Augustijnen, January 2013

SVEN AUGUSTIJNEN
born in 1970 in Mechelen, Belgium
lives in Brussels, Belgium

Spectres

2011
single-screen video projection, dimensions variable,
screen ratio 16:9
DVD, colour, stereo audio
1 hr. 43 min. 8 sec.
this work is number one from an edition of three
plus one artist's proof
inv. no. MZ000067

Provenance
acquired from Jan Mot, Brussels, in 2011

Exhibited
Sven Augustijnen: Spectres, WIELS, Brussels,
8 May – 31 July 2011 (another example exhibited).
Sven Augustijnen 'Spectres', Kunst Halle Sankt Gallen,
13 Aug. – 9 Oct. 2011 (another example exhibited).
The Idea of Africa (Re-invented) #3:
Sven Augustijnen – Spectres, Kunsthalle Bern,
8 Oct. – 27 Nov. 2011 (another example exhibited).
Sven Augustijnen 'Spectres', de Appel arts centre,
Amsterdam, 15 Oct. 2011 – 12 Feb. 2012
(another example exhibited).

Awards
Evens Arts Prize, 2011
Prix du Groupement National des Cinémas
de Recherche, 2011
Prix des Médiathèques, 2011
special mention FIDMarseille Grand Prix de la
Compétition Internationale, 2011

Literature
Sven Augustijnen, 'Qu'en pensez-vous Bwana Kitoko?',
in: *A Prior,* no. 14, Ghent, 2007, pp. 6 – 144.
Sven Augustijnen, ed., *Spectres,* ASA Publishers,
Brussels, 2011.
Matthias De Groof, 'Spectres', in: *Rekto:verso,*
Summer 2011, http://www.rektoverso.be/artikel/
spectres.
T.J. Demos, *Sven Augustijnen's Spectropoetics,* ASA
Publishers, Brussels, 2011.
Lars Kwakkenbos, 'Spectres', in: *Sven Augustijnen.*
Spectres. World Premiere, Kunstenfestivaldesarts,
Brussels, 2011, pp. 4 – 17.
Pieter Van Bogaert, 'Of zien we spoken?
"Spectres" – Sven Augustijnen in Wiels',

in: *<H>art,* no. 81, Antwerp, 12 May 2011, p. 3
(illustrated in colour).
Roland Van de Sompel, 'Part of the process.
What a day for a daydream', in: *Mousse,* no. 27,
Feb. – March 2011, pp. 58 – 63 (illustrated in colour).
Stefaan Vervoort, 'De onvolledige waarheid.
Spectres van Sven Augustijnen', in: *Metropolis M,*
Oct. – Nov. 2011, pp. 70 – 73 (illustrated in colour).

L'Histoire Belge

2007
ten offset prints on paper, individually framed
overall: 75.5 × 245.5 cm; each print, incl. frame:
36.5 × 47 cm
this work is number five from an edition of five
plus two artist's proofs
inv. no. K002786

Provenance
acquired from Jan Mot, Brussels, in 2008

Exhibited
Sven Augustijnen. L'Histoire Belge, Jan Mot, Brussels,
9 Nov. – 22 Dec. 2007 (another example exhibited).
Weder entweder noch oder, Württembergischer
Kunstverein Stuttgart, 31 May – 3 Aug. 2008
(another example exhibited).
Sven Augustijnen. L'Histoire Belge, PMMK, Ostend,
27 Sept. – 25 Dec. 2008.
Report on Probability, Kunsthalle Basel,
28 June – 30 Aug. 2009 (another example exhibited).
The State of Things. Brussels / Beijing, BOZAR,
Brussels, 18 Oct. 2009 – 10 Jan. 2010.

Literature
Björn Scherlippens, 'Interview met Sven Augustijnen',
in: Björn Scherlippens, Claire Van Damme, Marijke
Van Eeckhaut and Patrick Van Rossem, eds., *Behind*
or Beside You. Dynamische processen in de coulissen
van de hedendaagse kunstschepping, Academia Press,
Ghent, 2009, pp. 71–76 (illustrated in colour).

Ann Veronica Janssens

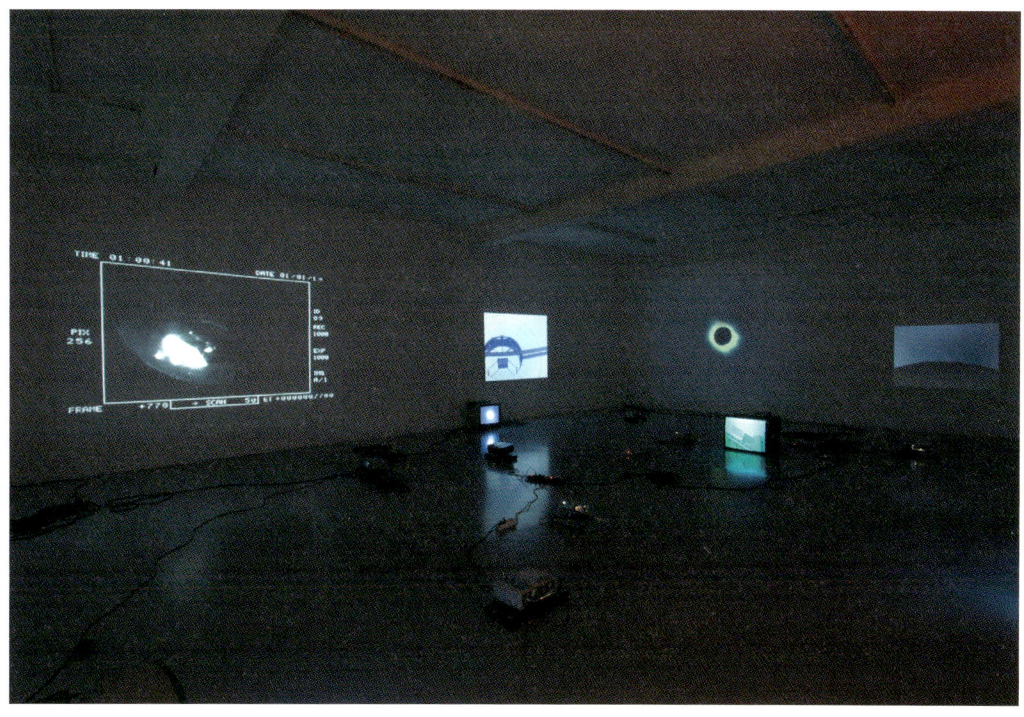

Riffs, 2008
installation view Galerie Micheline Szwajcer, Antwerp

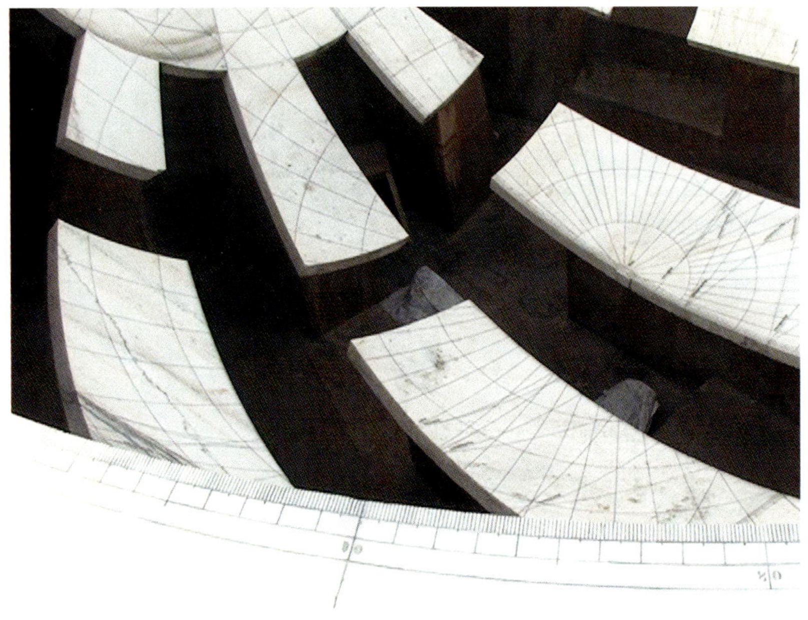

Jai Prakash Yantra [video still], 2008

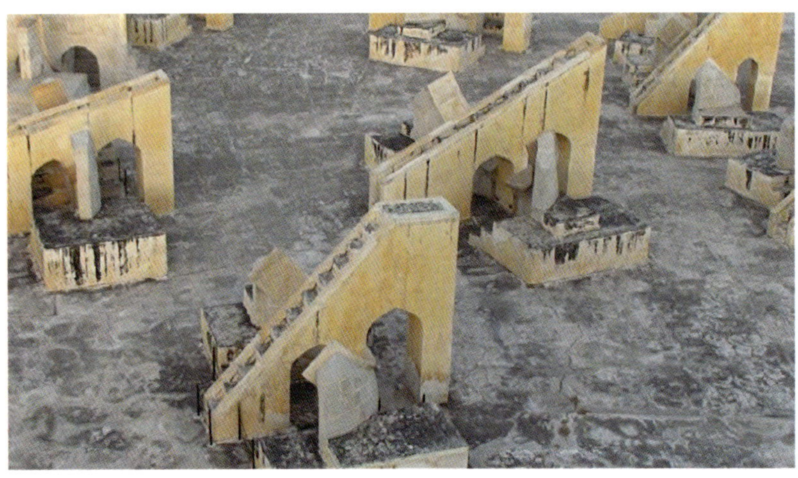

Lever du jour à Jantar Mantar [video still], 2008

RIFFS

The installation *Riffs* brings together thirteen videos in a
laboratory-like setting.
All the videos were made between 2006 and 2008. The
filming took place on different locations and in several
countries (among others: the observatory Jantar Mantar
in India, the Turkish village of Side, the solar furnaces
in Odeillo and Font-Romeu in France, and the university of
Louvain-la-Neuve in Belgium).
The videos all deal with the subject of light and the stars.
They feature measuring equipment, that by its architectural,
sculptural or experimental nature resonates with certain
models of modern and contemporary art.

Ann Veronica Janssens

Looking for the Pole Star [video stills], 2008

This video tracks the slow rise of the twilight. It was shot at Jantar Mantar, from the basis of Dhruva Darshak Yantra, an astronomical observation instrument that is used for identifying the North Star.

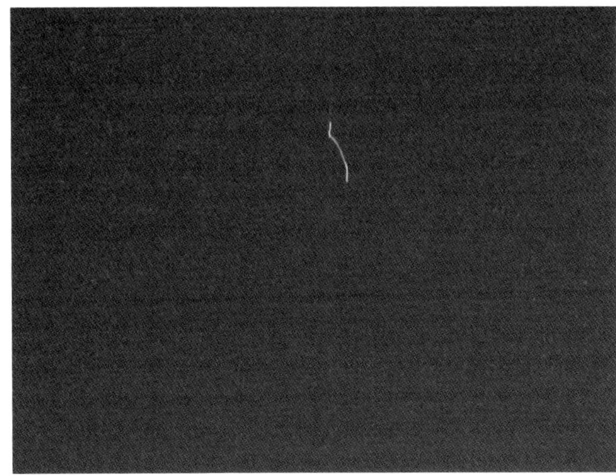

Jupiter [video stills], 2008

A drawing, caused by a moving camera that is filming
the brightness of the planet Jupiter.

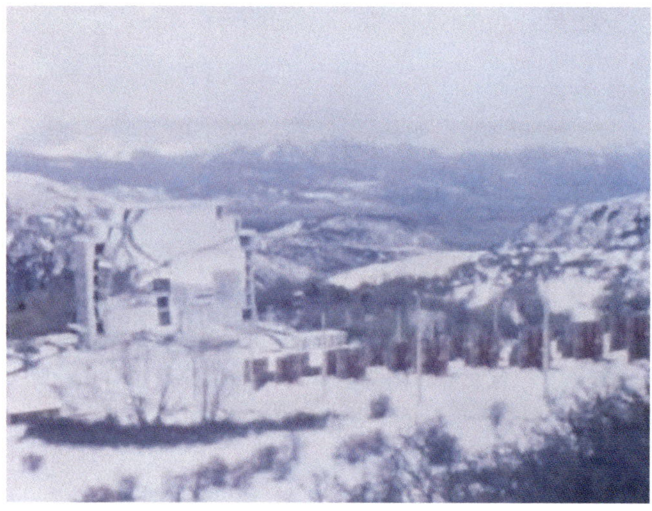

Odeillo (Super 8 mm version) [video still], 2008

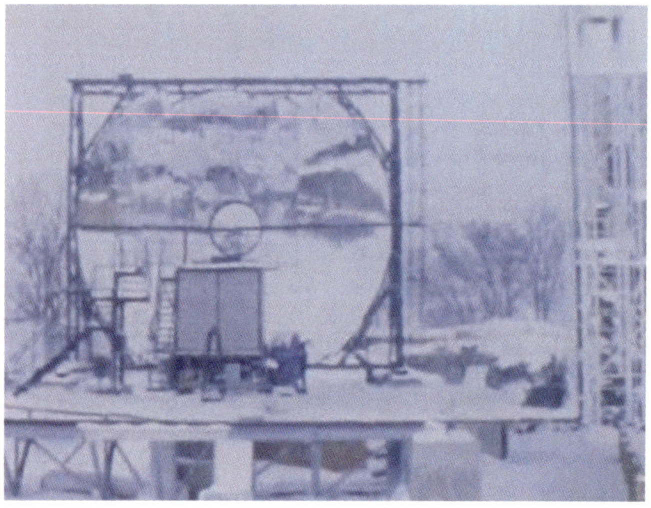

Font-Romeu [video still], 2008

Font-Romeu, a village near Odeillo, hosts the prototype that served to create Odeillo's solar furnace.
Nowadays, the inhabitants of Font-Romeu use this
prototype to bake bread and make ceramics.

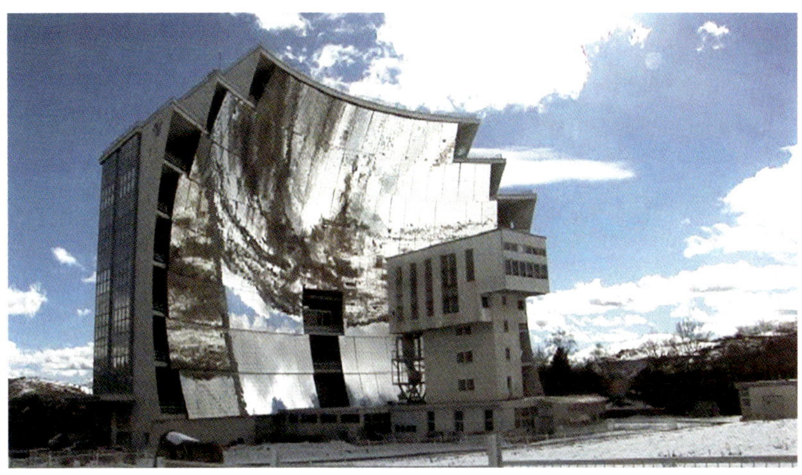

Odeillo (HD version) [video still], 2008

Odeillo, a village in the French Pyrenees, hosts an
exceptional solar furnace. A solar furnace is a structure used to harness sunlight in order to produce high
temperatures, usually for industry purposes. This
is achieved by using a curved mirror (or an array of
mirrors) that acts as a parabolic reflector, concen-
trating light onto a focal point. The solar furnace of
Odeillo employs an array of plane mirrors to gather
sunrays, reflecting them onto a larger curved mirror.
The rays are then focused onto an area that has the
size of a cooking pot and can reach up to 3000 °C.

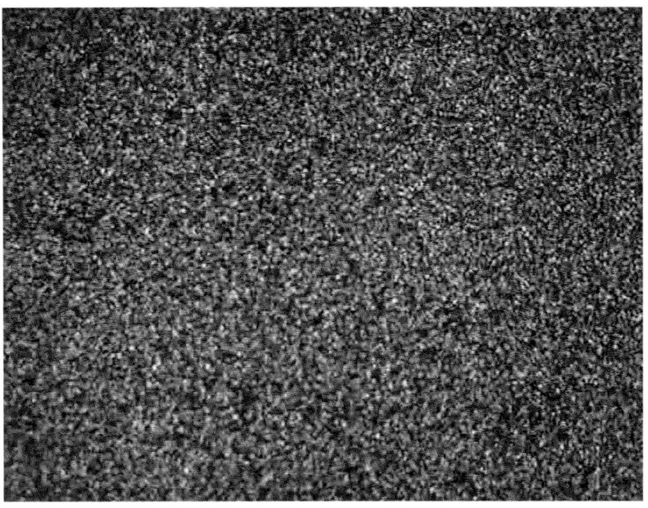

Neige cosmique [video still], 2008

Neige cosmique was produced in Brussels. It features static on a single-channel monitor.

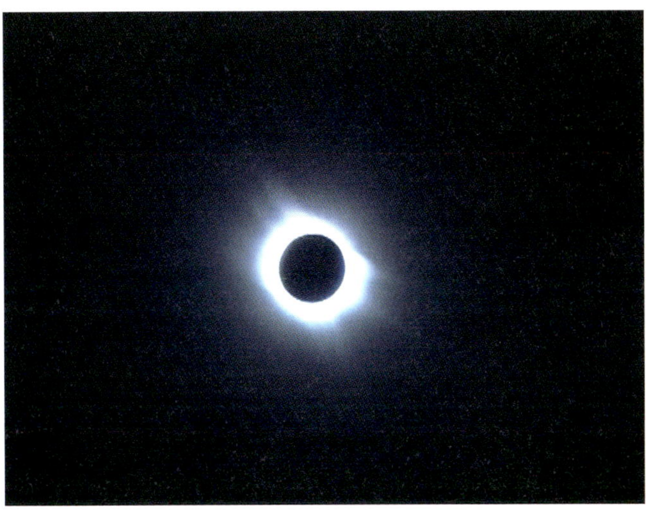

Side (natural version) [video still], 2006

Side (natural version) shows the solar eclipse of 29 March 2006. The video was shot in the city of Side, in Turkey.

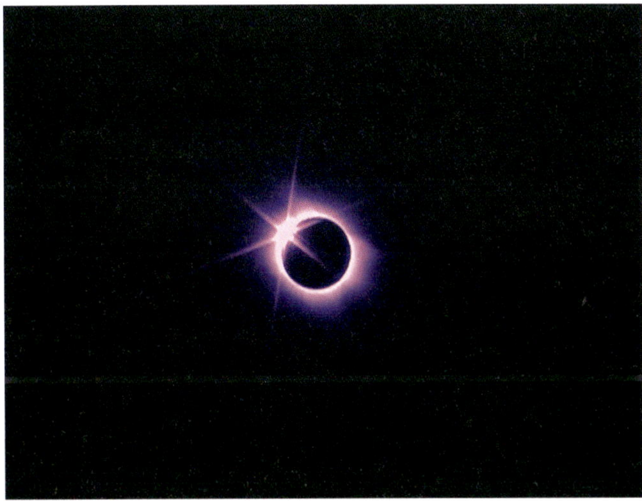

Side (studio version) [video still], 2006

Side (studio version) shows the solar eclipse of 29 March 2006. The video was shot in the Turkish city of Side and was later digitally colorized.

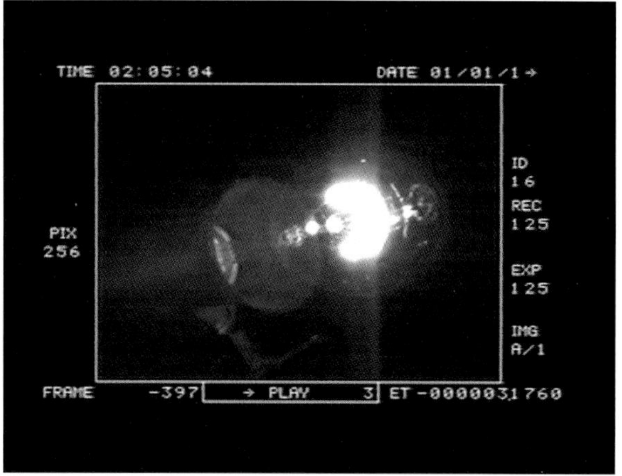

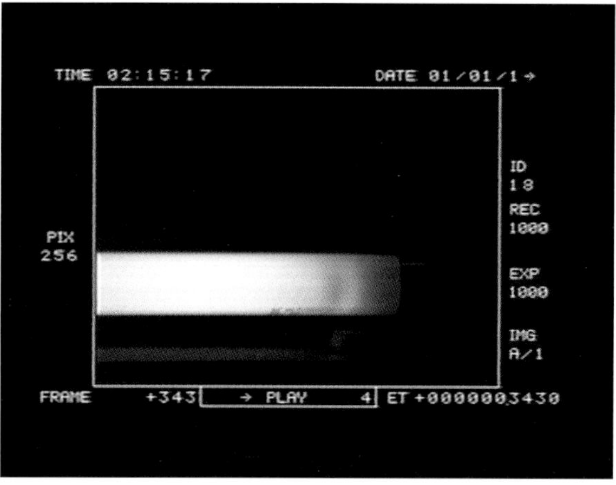

Slow light [video stills], 2007

Slow light features image captures of the switching
on of a 25 watt light bulb and a neon light, shot at
1000 frames a second. The video was made at the
Section of Thermodynamics at the university of
Louvain-la-Neuve.

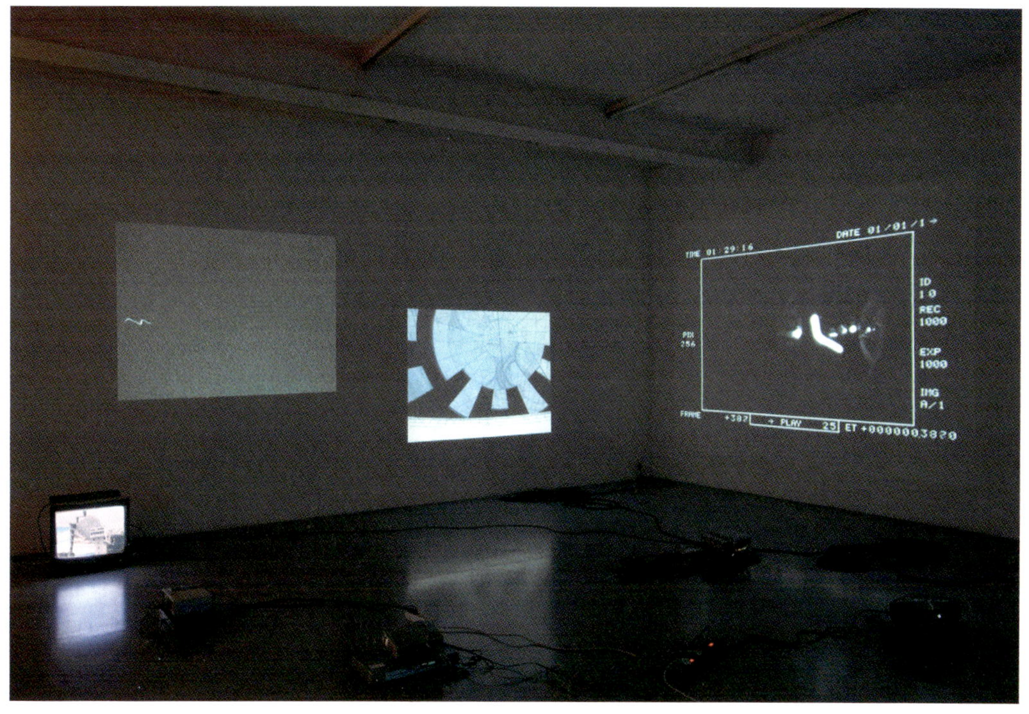

Riffs, 2008
installation view Galerie Micheline Szwajcer, Antwerp

ANN VERONICA JANSSENS
born in 1956 in Folkestone, United Kingdom
lives in Brussels, Belgium

Riffs

2008
thirteen parts –
part i: *Crépuscule à Jantar Mantar (Vénus)*
2008
single-monitor video installation, dimensions variable,
screen ratio 4:3 or 16:9
DVD, colour, mute
5 min. 13 sec.
part ii: *Font-Romeu*
2008
single-channel video projection, dimensions variable,
screen ratio 4:3
Super 8 mm film transferred to DVD, colour, mute
1 min. 25 sec.
part iii: *Jai Prakash Yantra*
2008
single-channel video projection, dimensions variable,
screen ratio 4:3
DVD, colour, mute
1 min. 28 sec.
part iv: *Jantar Mantar*
2008
single-channel video projection, dimensions variable,
screen ratio 4:3 or 16:9
DVD, colour, mute
2 min. 51 sec.
part v: *Jupiter*
2008
single-channel video projection, dimensions variable,
screen ratio 4:3 or 16:9
DVD, colour, mute
9 sec.
part vi: *Lever du jour à Jantar Mantar*
2008
single-monitor video installation, dimensions variable,
screen ratio 16:9
DVD, colour, mute
2 min. 8 sec.
part vii: *Looking for the Pole Star*
2008
single-channel video projection, dimensions variable,
screen ratio 4:3
DVD, colour, mute
17 min. 24 sec.
part viii: *Neige cosmique*
2008
single-monitor video installation, dimensions variable,
screen ratio 4:3

DVD, black and white, mute
7 min. 40 sec.
part ix: *Odeillo (HD version)*
2008
single-monitor video installation, dimensions variable,
screen ratio 4:3 or 16:9
DVD, colour, mute
4 min. 51 sec.
part x: *Odeillo (Super 8 mm version)*
2008
single-monitor video installation, dimensions variable,
screen ratio 4:3
Super 8 mm film transferred to DVD, colour, mute
2 min. 42 sec.
part xi: *Side (natural version)*
2006
single-monitor video installation, dimensions variable,
screen ratio 4:3
DVD, colour, mute
3 min. 33 sec.
part xii: *Side (studio version)*
2006
single-channel video projection, dimensions variable,
screen ratio 4:3
DVD and DV-PAL, colour, mute
3 min. 33 sec.
part xiii: *Slow light*
2007
single-channel video projection, dimensions variable,
screen ratio 4:3
DVD, black and white, mute
10 min. 55 sec.
video camera operator / assistant: Guillaume Bleret
this work is number one from an edition of three plus
one artist's proof
inv. no. K002800

Provenance
acquired from Galerie Micheline Szwajcer, Antwerp,
in 2009

Exhibited
Galerie Micheline Szwajcer, Antwerp,
30 Oct. – 6 Dec. 2008 (another example exhibited).
0034 93 487 64 02, Galeria Toni Tàpies, Barcelona,
29 Jan. – 27 March 2009 (another example
exhibited).

Literature
Experienced, BasePublishing, Brussels, 2009
(illustrated in colour).
Serendipity, WIELS, Brussels, 2011
(illustrated in colour).

Ana Torfs

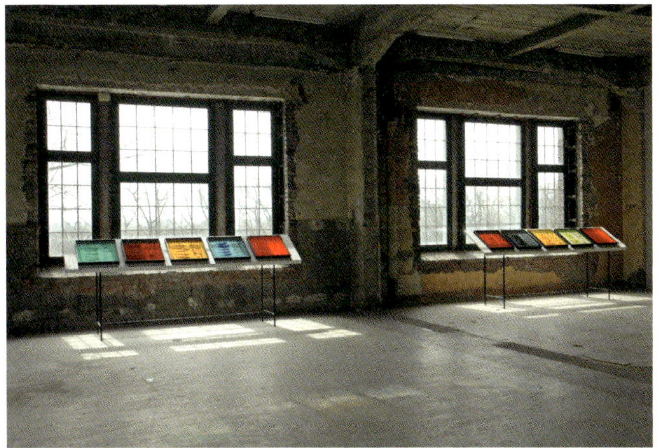

[...] STAIN [...], 2012
installation view *Manifesta 9*, Genk

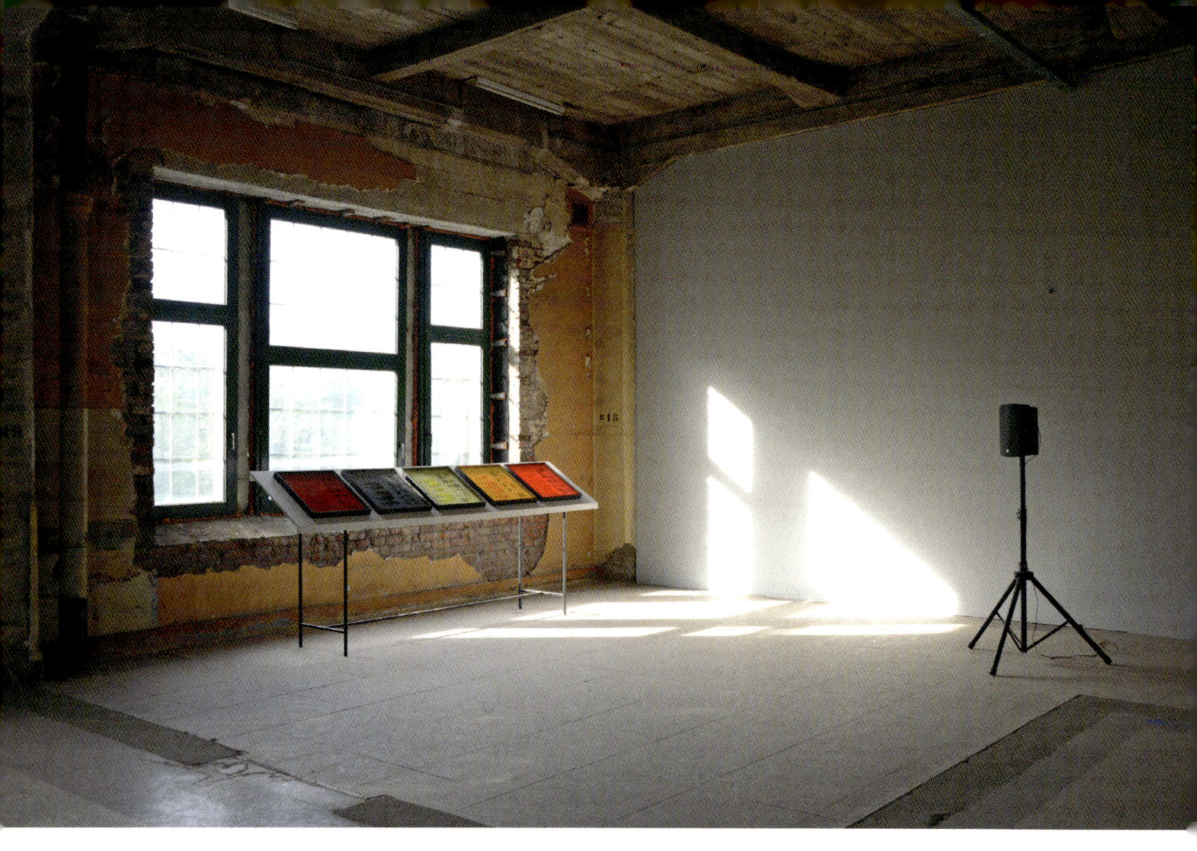

PRONTOSIL 2   *Prontosil resulted from research, directed by German chemist and pathologist Gerhard Domagk, on the antibacterial action of certain coal-tar dyes. In 1932 he was looking at a new red leather dye, which was commercially marketed by the Bayer division of I.G. Farben as Prontosil.*

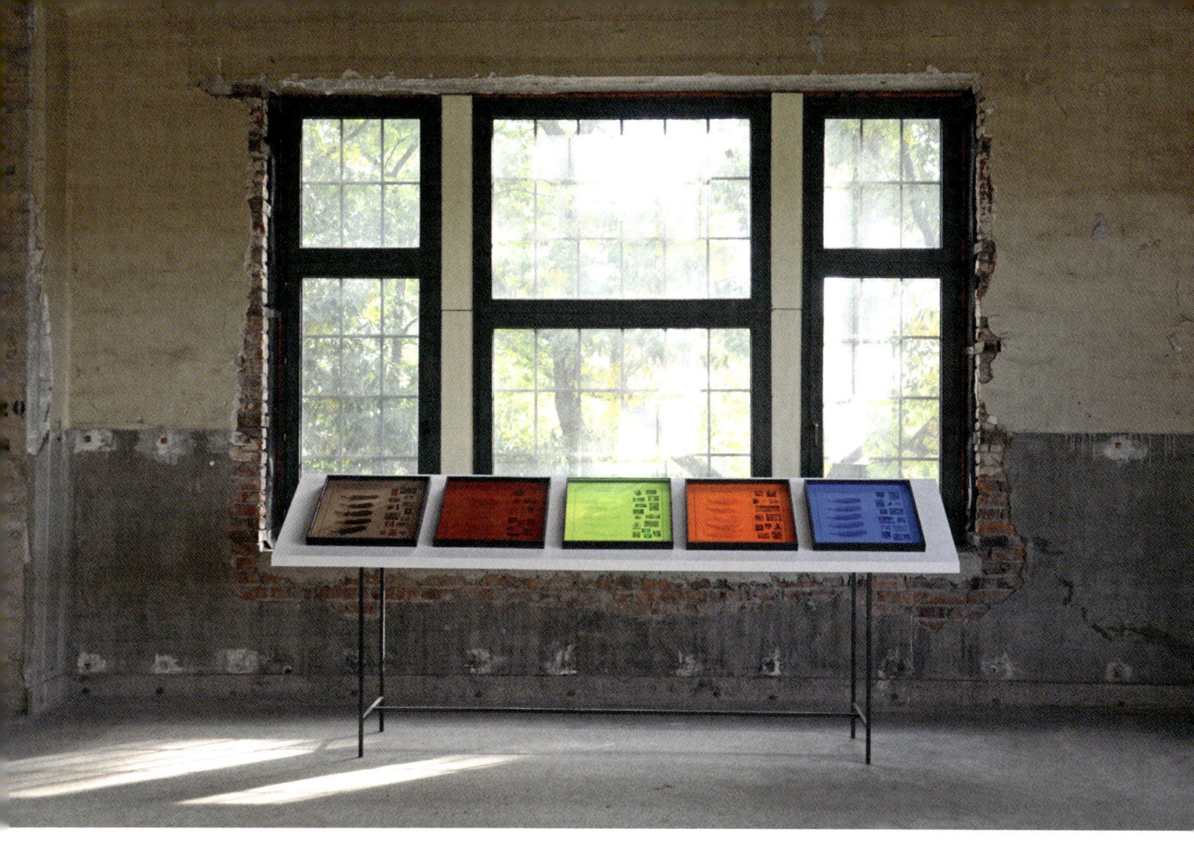

MALACHITE GREEN 4 *He witnessed the arrival, late, at a fashionable first night, of Oscar Wilde wearing "a large carnation of a violent green." The Artist, in its April issue, told you how to make your own: "Take a white carnation by plunging the stem in an aqueous solution of the coal-tar dye called malachite green."*

MAUVE

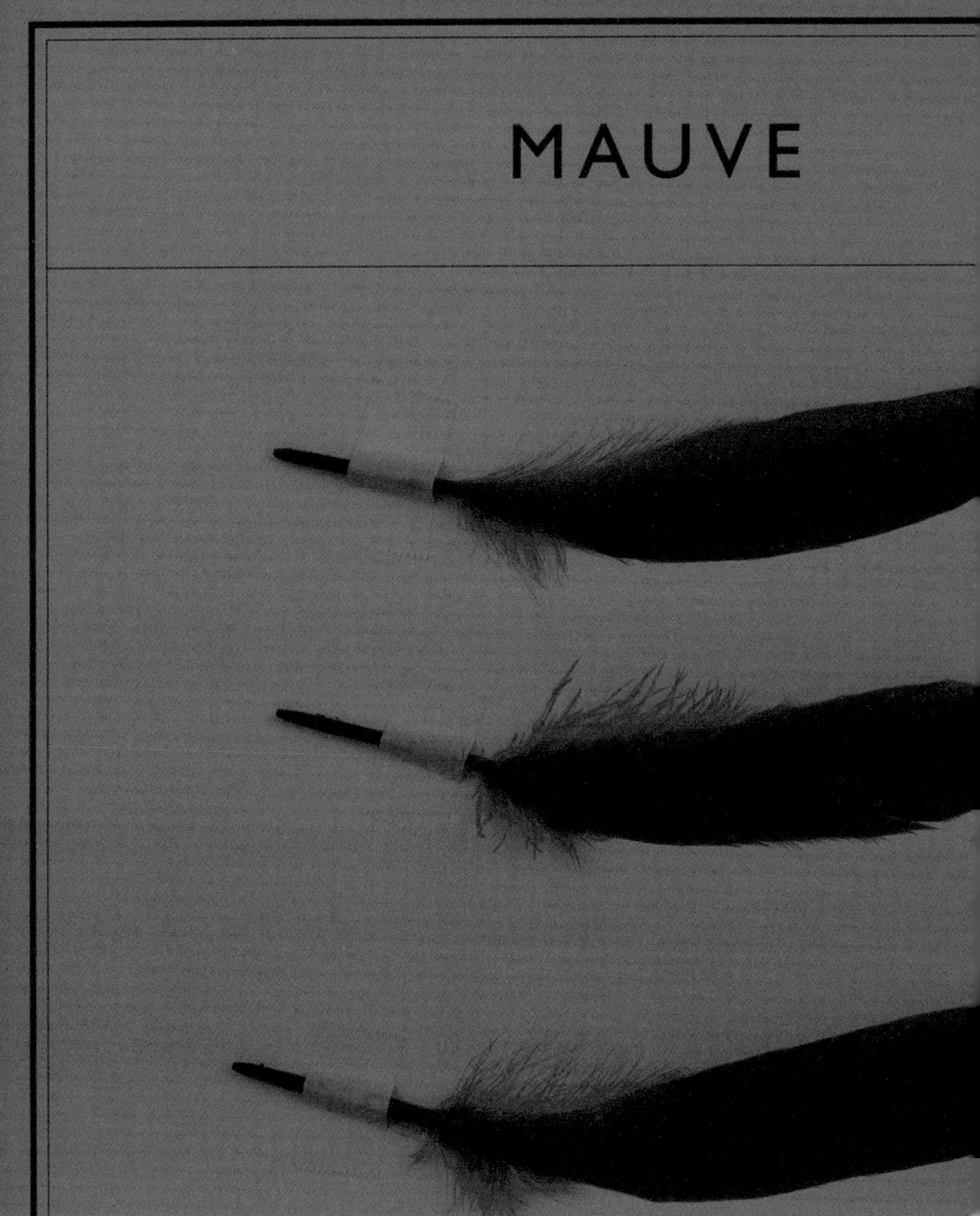

TARTRAZINE 2   *You might pass up a macaroni and cheese that contains the slightly foreboding-sounding tartrazine.*

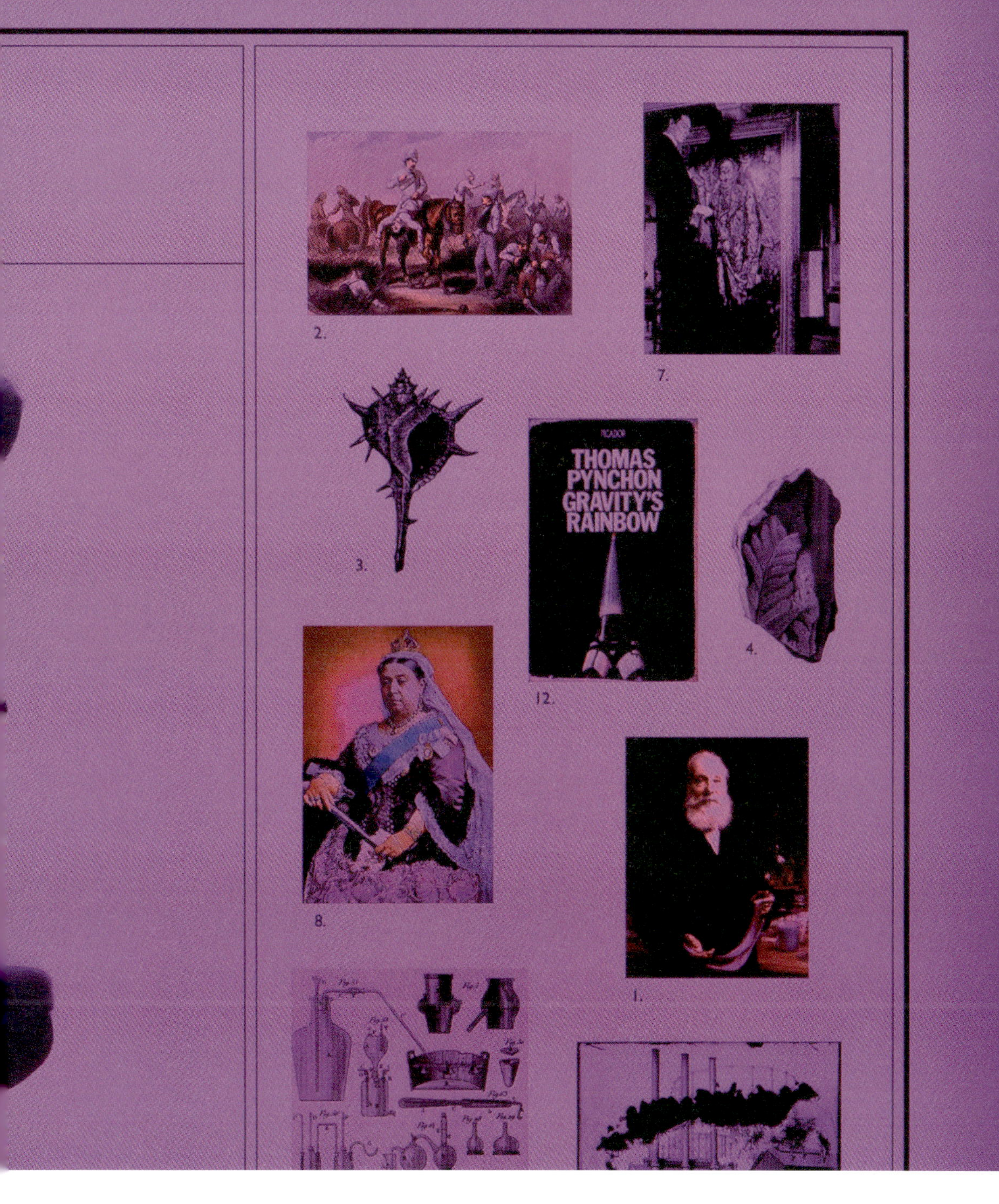

METHYLENE BLUE 6   *At Schweitzer's heels are usually his dogs, splashed with the methylene blue that is used to combat the prevalent skin diseases.*

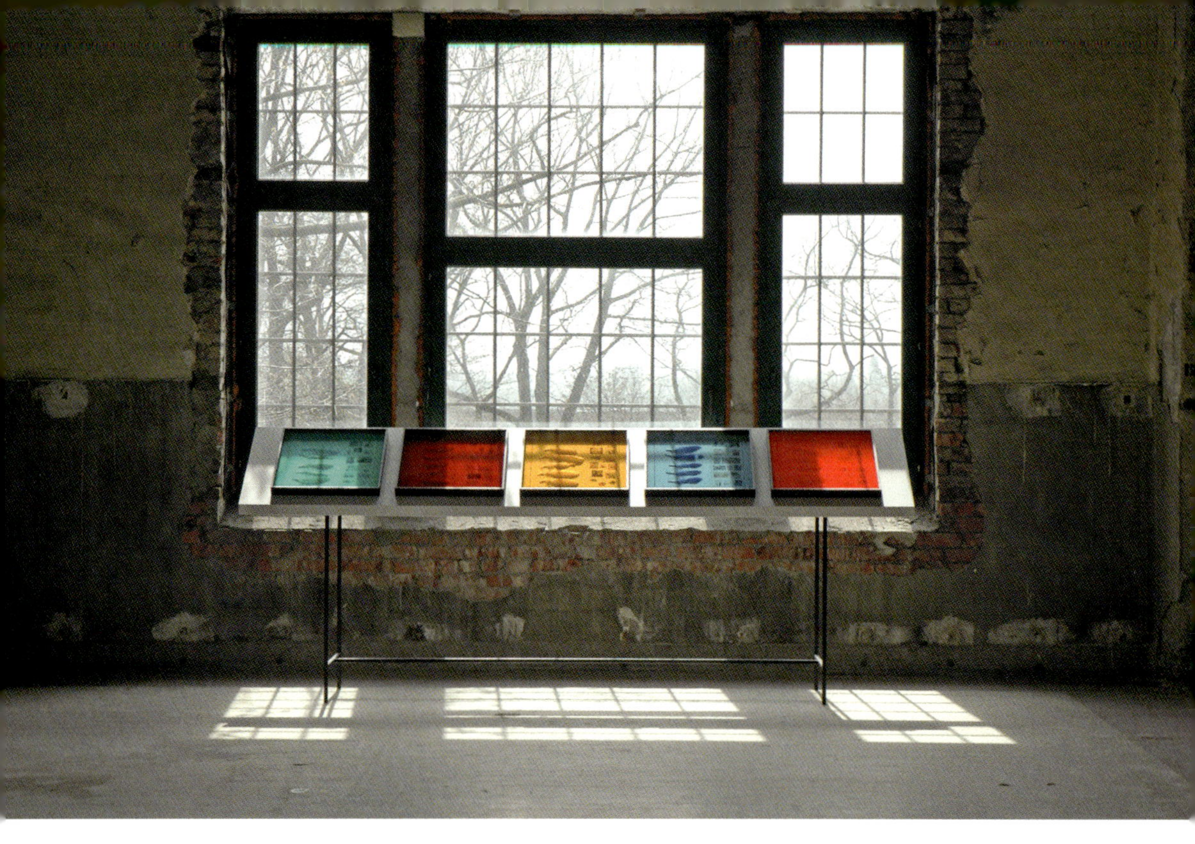

BISMARCK BROWN 4   *Gardeners have a Bismarck rose and a giant Bismarck strawberry, and the fashionable world attires itself in Bismarck brown.*

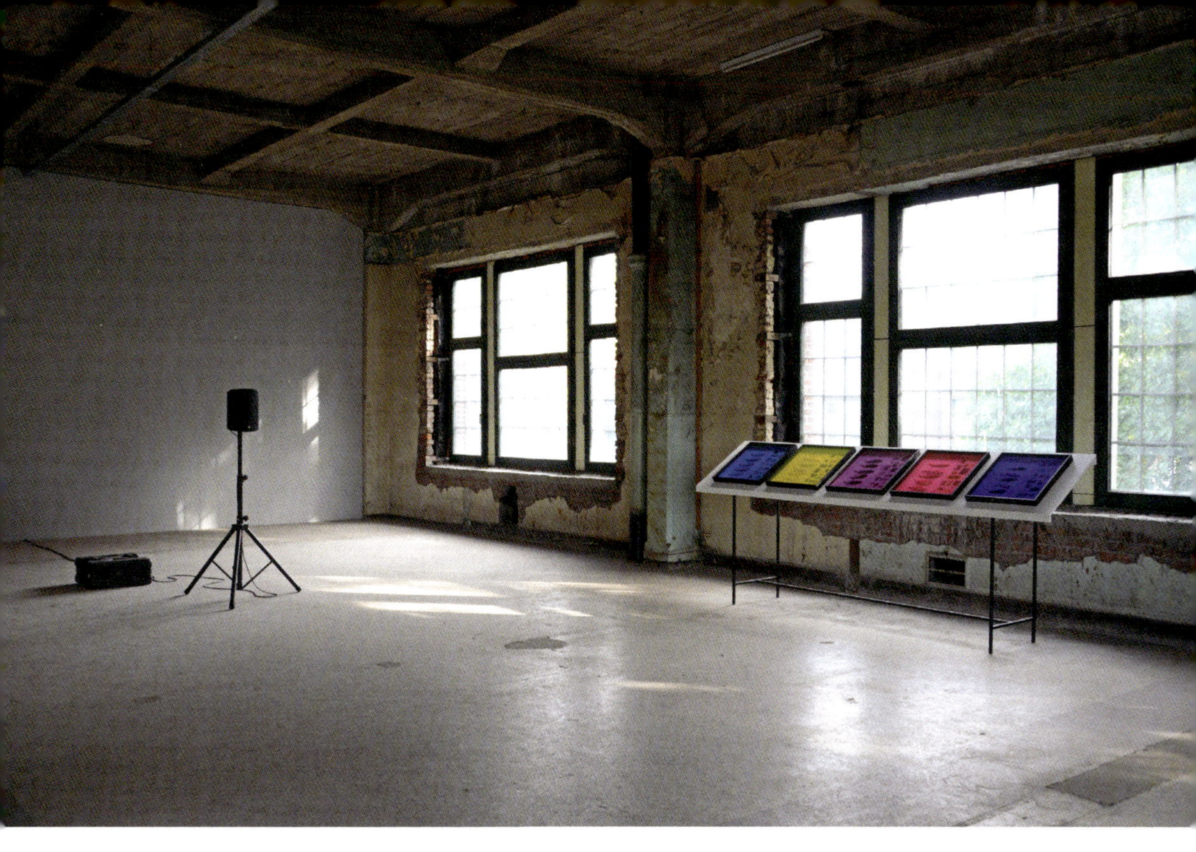

INDIGO 5   The central role played by India is captured in the word indigo. Although the Sanskrit term for indigo came from nila, meaning dark blue — which survives in our word, aniline — the ancient Greeks referred to the product as indikon, the Indian dye.

URANIN 3   *A small amount of uranin, injected in the back of a person's ear, will show up in the eye and on the lips in a few seconds if he is alive. It is particularly useful on the battlefield, to tell actual death from apparent death.*

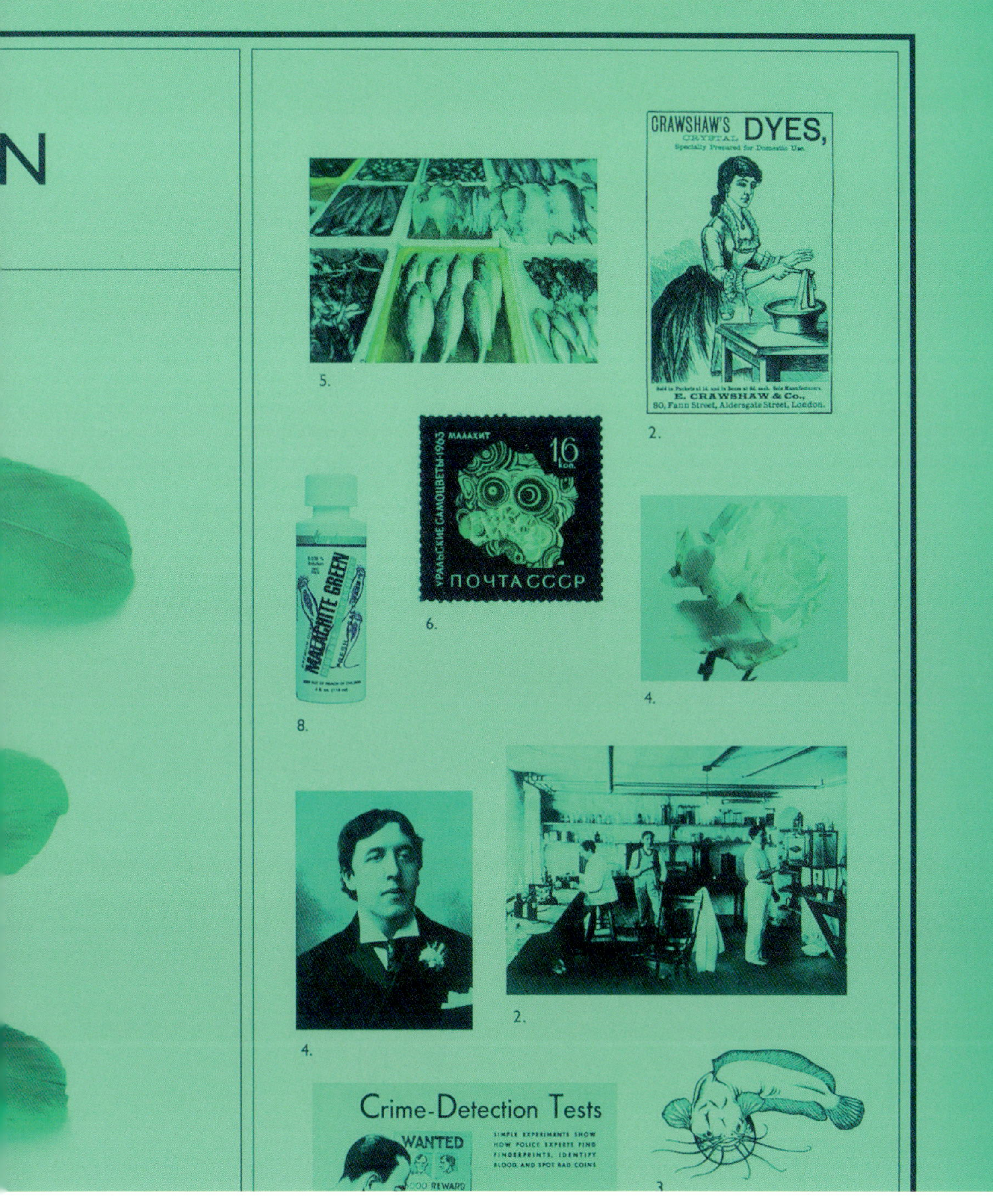

CONGO RED 5 *Congo red was introduced into Japan in 1886. Japanese merchants soon began advertising garments coloured with Congo red or related coal-tar dyes, as symbols of modernization and progress.*

[…] STAIN […]

In English the noun 'stain' and the verb 'to stain' have various meanings.
It is a reference to colour, but also to spots or dirt, and figuratively
to a 'blemish', as in: 'a stained reputation'. The […] is a familiar punctua-
tion mark, the so-called ellipsis. It means something was left out. In
that sense it also refers to the 'gaps' between the sentences in the sound
recording, which is part of the installation. Finally it is an indirect
reference to the quotes, or the existing texts and / or images, which
I often work with. *[…] STAIN […]* is meticulously assembled from found
images and texts: a collage or montage.

From a distance a strolling visitor will see monochrome coloured sur-
faces on white tables. As the visitor approaches the work, his perception will change. He will clearly distinguish black wooden frames
with coloured acrylic glass. Standing in front of the tables, a second
layer behind the transparent glass becomes apparent: a print with the
name of a colour in huge letters in the upper left-hand corner, with
goose feathers glued underneath and a series of numbered images—
engravings, paintings and various reproductions—in a column on the
right (similarly to an old encyclopaedia).

Synthetic dyes are the starting point for this installation. The explosion
of colours we have known since 1856 was only possible through the
commercial use of the waste products of coke manufacture, such as
coal tar. It is almost as if the ancient dream of the alchemist is realized:
instead of creating gold out of lead, all the colours of a rainbow were
produced from the darkest black of coal tar.

In 1856 the 18-year-old English chemistry student William Henry Perkin
patented a purple dye, mauve, which he distilled from coal tar. Perkin
discovered the dye by coincidence, when he was looking for a synthetic
variant of quinine, in the fight against malaria. Mauve was the first
mass-produced synthetic dye. The creation of mauve resulted in the
emergence of big chemical companies. Bayer, BASF, as well as
AGFA, all set out as dye manufacturers, during the second half of the
nineteenth century. The research on synthetic dyes from coal tar in-
duced many other discoveries and was crucial for the development of
explosives, medicines and pesticides.

At the end of World War I a number of German chemical concerns, such as BASF, Bayer, AGFA and Hoechst, united themselves as IG Farben (in German 'Farben' means both 'colour' and 'paint'), which was to become the core of Hitler's war industry…
I chose twenty representative synthetic dyes, with such evocative names as 'Congo red', 'Bismarck brown', 'Paris violet' and 'uranin', and searched for connected images, each image bearing a number. The captions referring to those numbered images appear to be missing, but I integrated them into the sound recording, which is part of the installation. A female voice reads out the names of the twenty selected colours and the 182 numbered captions in an artificial tone, played in random order by a computer programme, with long silences between each 'caption'. Some colours—'rose Bengal', for instance, first produced in 1882— are still in use today, whereas historic 'mauve', from 1856, is no longer produced.
For the layout of the twenty prints I drew inspiration from an amazing colour sample catalogue from Friedrich Bayer's dye factory, dating from 1910, in which goose feathers, in all the colours of the rainbow, provided an overview of the dyes Bayer was producing at the time.

Ana Torfs

ANA TORFS
born in 1963 in Mortsel, Belgium
lives in Brussels, Belgium

[...] STAIN [...]

2012
installation consisting of:
(i) four tables made of MDF (painted white) and steel profiles (painted black)
each: 127.5 × 327.5 × 68.5 cm
(ii) twenty inkjet prints on paper, mounted on Dibond, with coloured goose
feathers (attached with acid free tape), wooden frames (painted black)
and coloured acrylic glass (3mm)
each: 53.5 × 53.5 × 4.5 cm
(iii) audio
two loudspeakers on tripods, a mixer, an amplifier, a Bässgen media player
with digital file on compact flash card, English voice (loop)
ca. 3 hr.
this work is number one from an edition of five plus one artist's proof
inv. no. MZ000116

Provenance
acquired directly from the artist in 2012

Exhibited
Manifesta 9, Genk, 2 June – 30 Sept. 2012.

Literature
Katerina Gregos, 'Ana Torfs', in: Cuauhtémoc Medina and Christopher Fraga,
eds., *The Deep of the Modern. A Subcyclopedia*, exh. cat., SilvanaEditoriale,
2012, pp. 240–241 and 262–265 (illustrated in colour).
http://catalog.manifesta9.org/en/torfs-ana/

Pieterjan Ginckels

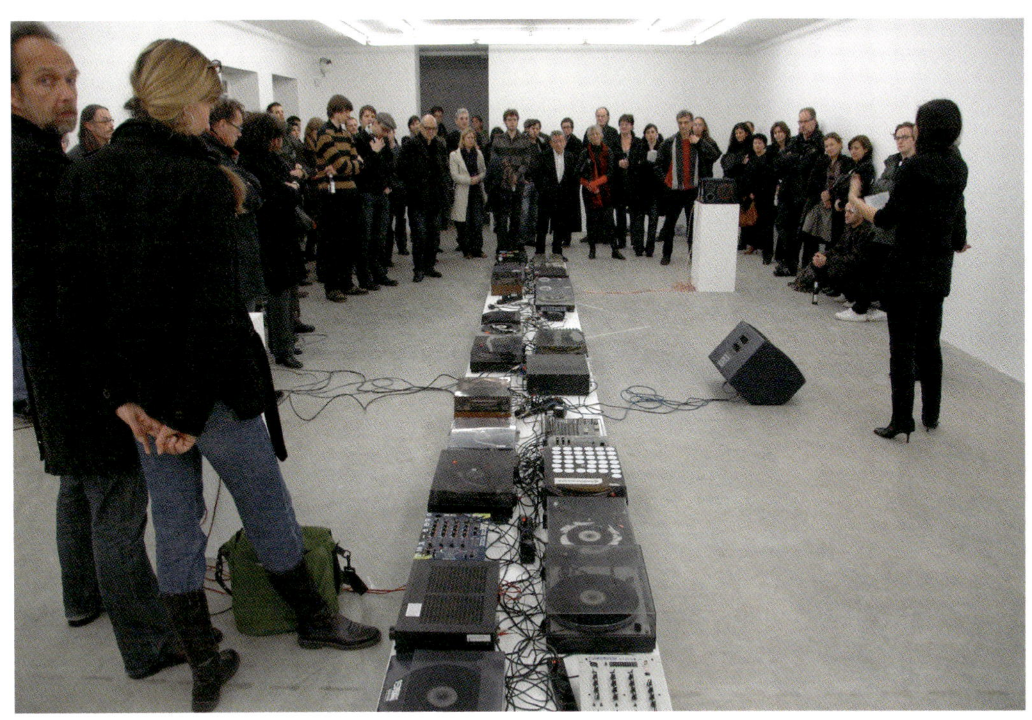

1000 Beats, 2008
installation view NAK, Aachen

PIETERJAN GINCKELS IN CONVERSATION WITH MIEKE MELS AND BJÖRN SCHERLIPPENS

Pieterjan Ginckels is thirty years old and has been active in the visual arts for just over ten years. His work hovers on the boundaries between performance, installation and conceptual art. Ginckels creates images closely connected to our daily world; the formal language he uses is both familiar and accessible. Music plays a significant role in his work. He is interested in the dynamic and collective character of the music industry, and translates this into images. In 2007, Ginckels created *1000 Beats* for the NAK in Aachen, an 'audio sculpture' that consists of turntables, amplifiers, speakers… as well as a vinyl record entitled *One Beat.* It is a key work in his oeuvre. For the first time, he joined various elements in an installation in which image, audio, and the involvement of the public take central place, aspects which he has in the meantime further explored in more recent projects. The installation was already on view at the Galleria Klerkx in Milan, at the Pluto Festival in Opwijk, at WIELS in Brussels, at De Brakke Grond in Amsterdam and at Mu.ZEE in Ostend. Mu.ZEE acquired this work—with its accompanying protocol—in 2011.

Björn Scherlippens: Let's start with the record. Music has always been part of your life, not only as a DJ but also with Nononoise, a project in which you involved your friends, primarily to make music. Later, you became interested in creating images as well. Was the vinyl record a logical step in this direction?

Pieterjan Ginckels: In my visual work, I try to generate energy the way I often experience it through music, concerts, labels, remixes, fans, festivals, even merchandising. A vinyl record is an ideal link in that sense. It is a sculpture and simultaneously also a carrier for something else. The grooves have been 'sculpted' in a technical manner. A locked groove is an even more interesting sculptural given; technical skill must be mastered in order to create a perfect loop of exactly 1.3 seconds. Not only the sculptural aspect is interesting, but the music itself as well. How do you decide what finally goes onto this kind of record and how do you create a dynamic in an exhibition? I didn't just want to make a record but saw the vinyl as an element in an installation that would be able to generate a certain dynamic. I approached *One Beat* as an artist, a perspective entirely different from that of a musician. In that capacity I started looking for partners to make the record with. I asked Cristian Vogel to make 1.3 seconds of music. The design studio Grandpeople made the design for the cover. I had been following the studio for a while and was only familiar with them from their designs of record sleeves for Scandinavian labels. The album was a good excuse to approach them; not as fan, but as an artist.

What exactly did you ask them? Did you steer them in a certain direction?
I asked them if they wanted to collaborate on an album I would use in an installation that would be called *1000 Beats.* I had a pretty good idea of what I wanted to do with the installation. Both Grandpeople and Cristian Vogel knew that it would consist of various borrowed turntables that together would make up a spatial sculpture. This context gave Cristian enough information to know what kind of sound waves and which manipulations he could use to create the widest possible spectrum when the fragment is spun out, sped up, or slowed down and given more bass or pitch. Grandpeople saw the record the way I do, as a sculpture, and created a design with a wink to Op art. The studio made a number of proposals from which I selected the design with the diamond. *1000 Beats* is an installation that consists of various facets and fragments. Together, the lines and dots create the illusion of a diamond and that idea appealed to me.

Aside from their contribution to the vinyl record, did they also provide input for the further development of the installation?
Cristian was very interested in this aspect but we haven't been able to set up the installation together yet. I would love it if this could work out, but apart from that, the installation offers numerous opportunities to involve other people in the project. At the very first presentation of *1000 Beats* at the NAK I invited Hans Nieswandt to fine-tune the installation. Nieswandt is a German music producer and DJ who really fascinates me. Among other things, he publishes records with Whirlpool Productions—*From disco to disco* (1996) was a worldwide hit. I asked him to tune the installation like an instrument, to the point where it would sound good to him. The setup at Mu.ZEE I realised with DJs Kong and Gratts. I had asked them to come and spin some records during the opening. Instead of using their own DJ set, I invited them to make music with my installation and the thirty turntables that were displayed. The performance began in silence, but after the opening speeches, the two DJs each set to work on a row of turntables which they activated from

left to right with a record of choice, playing various genres from jazz and disco to soul… The records sounded only as good as the turntables they were played on. After each song, the DJs went on to the next player and I put on a copy of *One Beat* that started playing in a loop. Their music eventually had to give way to *One Beat,* right up to when their last album ended and all you could hear was *1000 Beats.* The last record playing had a great impact and when that melody faded, the rhythm of the work changed completely. It was what I would call a 'turn-in performance'.

Mieke Mels: Why do you invite someone else every time to tune the sound to the room?

The way sound 'sounds good' in a space, is to some extent a personal choice. A bass freak, for example, will turn up all the basses. I see these collaborations primarily as an opportunity to involve someone else in my work. Since that person has to make decisions about my work, he is giving input as well. By inviting others, I involve them directly in the exhibition area and this creates an afterlife for the installation. The works are 'lived', which is actually very meaningful in the context of the exhibition space.

That contribution also consists of inviting the audience to lend out their turntables.

That's right. For the first setup at NAK I turned to the audience. I used my own network—friends, family, colleagues—and the institution's network. I brought my own material and there was the NAK's equipment. Whether an old Dual or a new Technics, every record player was welcome; in a way each piece, through its unique shape and sound, represented the various lenders. This diversity enhanced the sound effect that had already been worked into the record. This approach, however, is not 'fixed'. In any future arrangement, I could very well set to work with only professional DJ equipment or create a very orderly setup with identical turntables.

At the NAK, did you already include some kind of return?

Yes, afterwards, everyone who participated was given the record that was played on their player. The number of records is limited, and they are only distributed through participation in *1000 Beats.* That's how the records are systematically spread all over the world.

After NAK, in 2009, you set up *1000 Beats* in the Galleria Klerkx in Milan. Did you round up the equipment in a different way?
I drove to Milan by car and had launched an appeal to friends and family. I planned to pick up the equipment on my way to Milan and bring it back after the exhibition. All along the drive from my studio in Aalst, to friends in Brussels and Leuven, family in Tienen and friends in Stuttgart, I steadily filled my car with turntables and speakers. When I arrived in Milan, I had a complete *1000 Beats* in my car.

This second arrangement was much more compact than the one at NAK?
Yes, it was much smaller. All the equipment had to fit in my car and the gallery space itself was much smaller than the space in Aachen.

At WIELS you set up *1000 Beats* in the context of *Short Tracks,* a cluster of 24 solo exhibitions in which each artist was given half an hour to exhibit. What was that like?
The idea was to build, exhibit and take down the installation within the duration of half an hour. The people who had responded to my call trickled in with their equipment, which they set up after the starting sign was given. The WIELS's PA systems were thrown into the mix as well, and their hum could be heard above the smaller speakers. This actually resulted in a new sound; the speed of the build-up of the installation was effectively audible! The whole was set up in the space in a much less stylized manner. We had five minutes—at most—to listen before the dismantling began. A very brief yet interesting version of *1000 Beats.*

At WIELS the focus was on the efficient process and less on the visual aspect. Does every space require a different spatial approach?
At NAK, it was the sequence of spaces in the building that influenced the setup. On the ground floor, there was an installation with video monitors on which I presented my *Stroboscope* movies: alternating black and white drawings which I play in sequence and at different speeds. The room was dark and those flashy line drawings reflected on the concrete floor and into the space. In the distance, *1000 Beats* was played as a kind of soundtrack, set up on the top floor.

The *Stroboscope* work is in that sense a natural counterpart of *1000 Beats.*
I felt that the relationship between the two levels was very important. The one work announced the other, as it were. On the stairs between the

two floors I had tagged my hitherto only self-portrait. *Ghost Appearance* (2007) is illuminated with black lights.

1000 Beats was set up as a catwalk in the middle of the rectangular space. Why this choice?
The majority of the record players stood on a low, long white pedestal on the floor, with a number of speakers strewn across the space like beacons. The catwalk, in a way, creates a central place for the lenders or audience, and makes it possible to walk around the work. *1000 Beats* sounds different, depending on the visitor's position. I placed a separate record player against the wall in a few places here and there. These were rather meant to function as form studies.

You donated a drawing that accompanies the installation to Mu.ZEE, a drawing depicting the structure of *1000 Beats.* Did you draw literal diagrams of how all the equipment is connected per setup?
Those diagrams have a practical use. They bring order to chaos and ensure the functioning of the installation. Together, these diagrams form a nice genealogy of every variant of *1000 Beats.* Usually I also add the initials of the owners of the units to the drawings of turntables, mixers and amplifiers.

The installation has been set up several times now. Every time, it includes the 'borrowing' of audio equipment. In what way did you incorporate this in the protocol that accompanied the purchase?
There are four components that act as constants in each setup: my own equipment, the equipment from my network, the equipment from the organisation and that of its network. That purchase drove me to think about these essential components in a very different way. Do I include my own equipment? What do I do with my network's equipment? I decided to finally make a last call to my network, not to lend equipment but to 'donate' it. A good argument was of course the fact that the equipment would become part of a museum collection. Together with my equipment, I put together a 'basic building kit' for *1000 Beats.*

What guidelines did you add to this?
Contacting the local network of the specific exhibition area is part of the work, and I have included this in the protocol. With each new setup, I am involved in the design of the sound and the installation. In the setup

at Mu.ZEE, the work was placed between two parallel walls on the ground floor. In a way, I closed that passage with the work, so it could be viewed and heard from both sides. It created a sort of *Bühne* effect. This is one possible setup but I have various scenarios in mind. *1000 Beats* could for instance become the soundtrack of a building. I would then connect a turntable, an amplifier and a loudspeaker to every electrical outlet in the exhibition spaces. It can also work in dialogue with the collection: how does the addition of this sound affect the experience of a specific work of art?

And the record? *One Beat* is published in a particular edition, and an edition is limited. How did you formulate this in the protocol? Every participating spectator who would normally take a record home after the show is now given something else in return. What that return consists of, is entirely determined by the museum. It could be, as is the case at Mu.ZEE, be a year's free entrance, for instance. The edition of

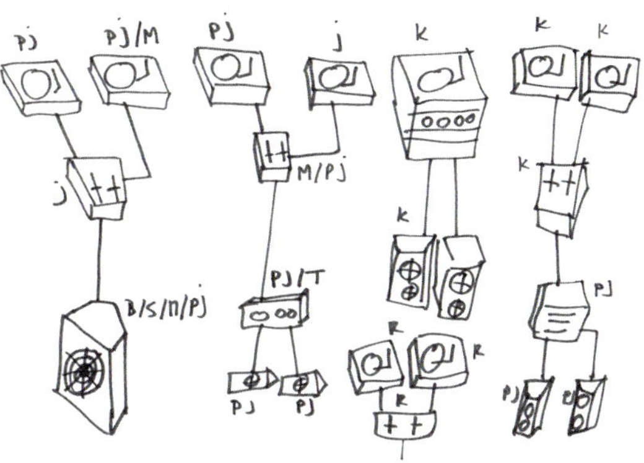

1000 Beats NAK, marker drawing, 2008

a record is limited but its playability isn't. You can play the life out of a record without affecting the sound; it does not disappear but only 'changes'… A worn-out *One Beat* is a new *One Beat.* Every sound is basically a good sound. You might as well say that the record becomes 'optimized' through use. In any case, it offers possibilities… After every setup, the time the records have been played is written down. In the next setup, I can use used or new records. But it is true that the work will eventually fade into a low hum. What most people do not know is that the B-side of the vinyl also contains beats. The grooves seem identical but Cristian Vogel has made a kind of foreshadowing of how he thought the installation could sound. He gave himself the freedom to create a three-minute soundscape using various modulations and different speeds. In this way, as an owner of the record, you also take the installation home.

Brussels, 16 November 2012

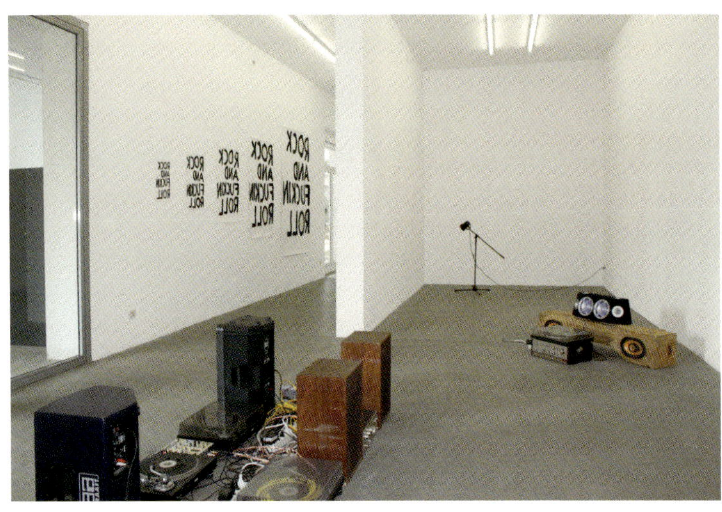

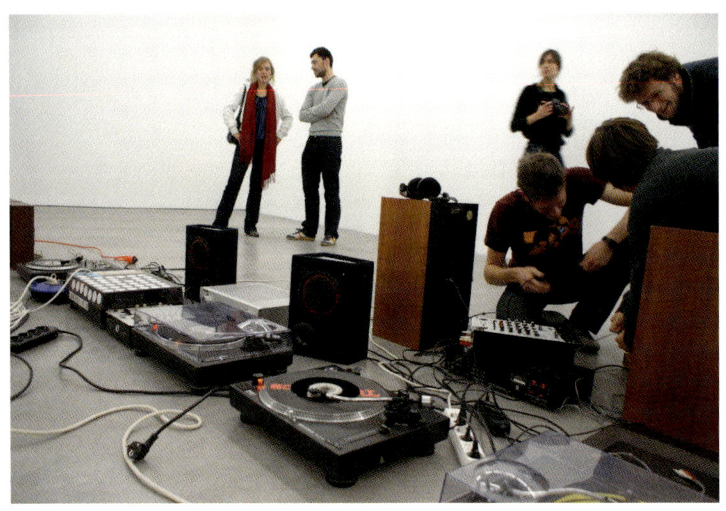

1000 Beats, 2008
installation view Galleria Klerkx, Milan (above)
and WIELS, Brussels (below)

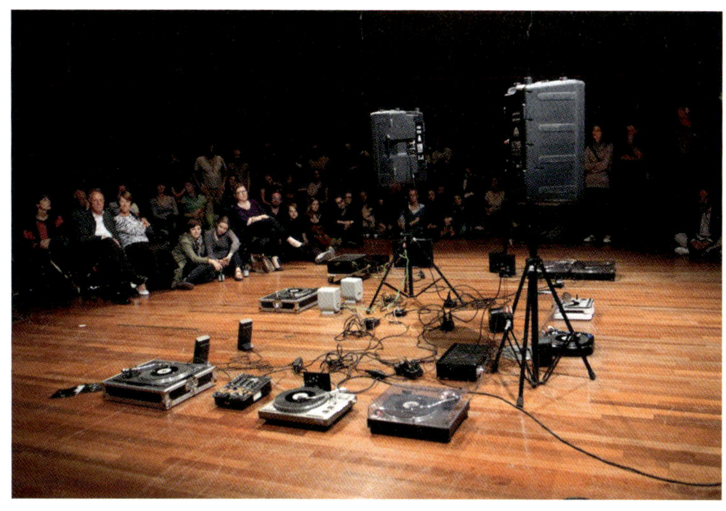

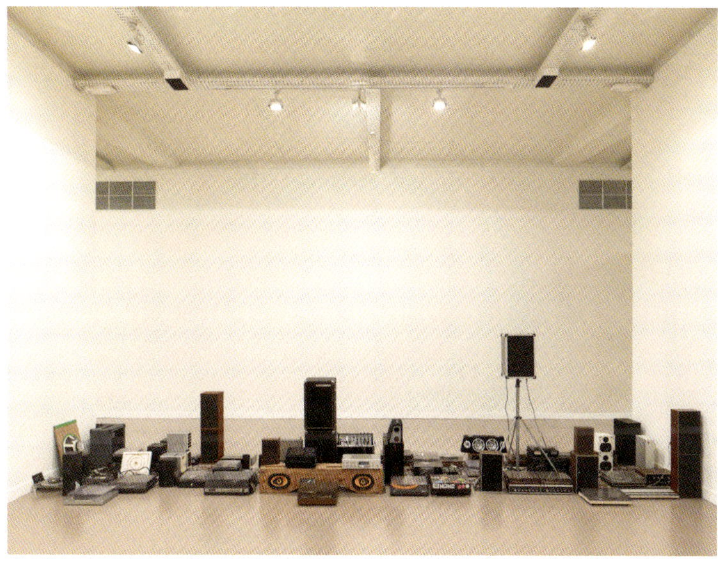

1000 Beats, 2008
installation view De Brakke Grond, Amsterdam
(above) and Mu.ZEE (below)

PIETERJAN GINCKELS
born in 1982 in Tienen, Belgium
lives in Brussels, Belgium

1000 Beats

2008
a variable number of turntables, amplifiers, mix panels, loudspeakers and
7-inch vinyl records *One Beat* (sleeve and label design by Grandpeople,
music by Cristian Vogel)
dimensions variable
inv. no. MZ000075

Provenance
acquired from Galerie de Expeditie, Amsterdam, in 2011

Exhibited
Pieterjan Ginckels – 1000 Beats, Mu.ZEE, Ostend,
20 Jan. – 19 Feb. 2012.
Performance Art Event, Vlaams Cultuurhuis de Brakke Grond, Amsterdam,
12 May 2011.
6daagse, Netwerk, Aalst,
28 Sep. – 3 Oct. 2010 (alternative version: *1000 Beats vs. Piste*).
Short Tracks, WIELS, Brussels,
3 Oct. 2009.
SONIC YOU, Galleria Klerkx, Milan,
18 Sept. – 12 Nov. 2009.
Pluto Festival, Nijdrop, Opwijk,
31 Oct. – 1 Nov. 2008.
Pieterjan Ginckels, Neuer Aachener Kunstverein, Aachen,
12 Jan. – 2 March 2008.

Literature
Pieterjan Ginckels, exh. cat., Neuer Aachener Kunstverein, Aachen, 2008
(illustrated in colour).

Index of Acquisitions
2007 – 2012

2007

Purchases

MARCEL BROODTHAERS
born in 1924 in Sint-Gillis, Belgium
died in 1976 in Cologne, Germany

Das Recht
1972
two silkscreen and offset prints
on cardboard
sheet i: 62 × 69 cm
sheet ii: 62 × 42.5 cm
this work is number thirteen from
an edition of one hundred and
twenty
acquired from mo-artgallery,
Amsterdam
inv. no. K002770

**MANON DE BOER AND
NEDJMA HADJ**
born in 1966 in Kodaikanal, India
lives in Brussels, Belgium
born in 1962 in Algiers, Algeria
lives in Brussels, Belgium

Villes Saisies / Captured Cities
2007
single-channel video projection,
dimensions variable,
screen ratio 4:3
DVD, colour, stereo audio
1 hr. 19 min. 39 sec.
this work is number one from an
edition of five plus two artist's
proofs
acquired from Jan Mot, Brussels
inv. no. K002771

**KOENRAAD DEDOBBELEER,
SOFIE HAESAERTS AND
COLOMBE MARCASIANO**
born in 1975 in Halle, Belgium
lives in Brussels, Belgium
born in 1972 in Leuven, Belgium

lives in Brussels, Belgium
born in 1974 in Massy, France
lives in Paris, France

**Pondering Nothing Much about
Even Less**
2006
two elements –
element i: single-channel slide
projection
eighty 35 mm slides, colour
dimensions variable
element ii: stool
painted wood
31 × 28 × 28 cm
acquired from Galerie Micheline
Szwajcer, Antwerp
inv. no. K002767

JAMES ENSOR
born in 1860 in Ostend, Belgium
died in 1949 in Ostend, Belgium

**[Poster for the Carnival in
Ostend]**
1931
lithograph on paper
47 × 32.5 cm
acquired from a Belgian private
collector
inv. no. SM002518

ERICH HECKEL
born in 1883 in Döbeln, Germany
died in 1970 in Radolfzell am
Bodensee, Germany

Zwei Matrosen
1916
woodcut on paper
35.5 × 28 cm
this work is from an edition of an
unknown size
acquired from Kunsthandel
Seghers-Vandepitte, Ostend
inv. no. SM002521

GUY MEES
born in 1935 in Mechelen, Belgium
died in 2003 in Antwerp, Belgium

Imaginair ballet
1998
nine elements – cut-outs of
coloured paper and textile,
watercolour on a sheet of paper
overall: ca. 140 × 310 × 5 cm
acquired from Galerie Micheline
Szwajcer, Antwerp
inv. no. K002769

Verloren ruimte
1990
three elements – cut-outs of
coloured paper
overall: ca. 100 × 197 × 5 cm
acquired from Galerie Micheline
Szwajcer, Antwerp
inv. no. K002768

LÉON SPILLIAERT
born in 1881 in Ostend, Belgium
died in 1946 in Brussels, Belgium

**Portrait de Marie Storck-
Hertoge**
1925
gouache and ink on paper
76 × 49 cm
acquired from a direct
descendant of Marie Storck-
Hertoge
inv. no. SM002523

Lapin
1917
lithograph on paper
sheet: 44 × 50 cm; image:
33.5 × 40 cm
this work is number three from
an edition of five (there also
exists an edition of twenty-five)
acquired from Kunsthandel
Seghers-Vandepitte, Ostend
inv. no. SM002522

JAN VERCRUYSSE
born in 1948 in Ostend, Belgium
lives in Brussels, Belgium

TOMBEAUX
1987
three elements – copper, lacquer

on wood, rosewood veneer on
wood
overall: 205 × 80 × 3.5 cm
top element: 70 × 50 × 0.5 cm
middle element: 30 × 80 × 2 cm
bottom element: 100 × 80 × 3.5 cm
acquired directly from the artist
inv. no. K002772

Gifts

LUC CLAUS
born in 1930 in Aalst, Belgium
died in 2006 in Brussels,
Belgium

Untitled
1975
ink on paper
58.5 × 46 cm
bequest from the artist
inv. no. K002778

Untitled
1980
graphite on paper
57 × 46 cm
bequest from the artist
inv. no. K002773

Untitled
1993
watercolour and ink on paper
58.5 × 46.5 cm
bequest from the artist
inv. no. K002780

Untitled
1994
watercolour and graphite
on paper
58.5 × 46.5 cm
bequest from the artist
inv. no. K002781

Untitled
1994
watercolour on paper
58 × 46 cm

bequest from the artist
inv. no. K002776

Untitled
1994
watercolour on paper
58.5 × 46 cm
bequest from the artist
inv. no. K002775

Untitled
2002
graphite on paper
66 × 45 cm
bequest from the artist
inv. no. K002782

Untitled
2003
graphite on paper
46.5 × 58.5 cm
bequest from the artist
inv. no. K002774

Untitled
n.d.
watercolour and graphite on
paper
58.5 × 46 cm
bequest from the artist
inv. no. K002779

Untitled
n.d.
watercolour and ink on paper
59.5 × 46 cm
bequest from the artist
inv. no. K002777

2008

Purchases

SVEN AUGUSTIJNEN
born in 1970 in Mechelen, Belgium
lives in Brussels, Belgium

L'Histoire Belge
2007
ten offset prints on paper,
individually framed
overall: 75.5 × 245.5 cm;
each print, incl. frame:
36.5 × 47 cm
this work is number five from an
edition of five plus two artist's
proofs
acquired from Jan Mot, Brussels
inv. no. K002786

JEAN BRUSSELMANS
born in 1884 in Brussels, Belgium
died in 1953 in Dilbeek, Belgium

[Beachscape with Bathers]
ca. 1935
oil, chalk and graphite on canvas
201 × 250 cm
acquired from the direct
descendants of the artist
inv. no. SM002528

ANOUK DE CLERCQ
born in 1971 in Ghent, Belgium
lives in Brussels, Belgium

Echo
2008
two elements –
element i: single-channel video
projection, dimensions variable,
screen ratio 16:9
DVD, black and white,
stereo audio
10 min. 32 sec.
element ii: digital print on

reflective paper
79 × 58 cm
this work is number ten from an
edition of thirteen
published by Museum
Dhondt-Dhaenens, Deurle
acquired from Museum
Dhondt-Dhaenens, Deurle
inv. no. K002788

LILI DUJOURIE
born in 1941 in Roeselare, Belgium
lives in Lovendegem, Belgium

Les illusions de la mémoire
2007
clay, black MDF, painted metal
96 × 152 × 97 cm
acquired directly from the artist
inv. no. K002784

Oostende
1974
nine-channel slide projection
nine 35 mm slides, colour
dimensions variable
acquired directly from the artist
inv. no. K002783

OLIVIER FOULON
born in 1976 in Brussels, Belgium
lives in Brussels, Belgium

**The Soliloquy of the Broom
[Amsterdam state]**
2008
two parts –
part i: single-channel film
projection, dimensions variable
16 mm film, colour
9 min. 32 sec.
part ii: four black and white inkjet
prints on paper, individually
mounted on a glass frame
overall: dimensions variable;
each frame: 60 × 50 cm
acquired directly from the artist
inv. no. K002787

FRANCISKA LAMBRECHTS
born in 1967 in Ninove, Belgium
lives in Brussels, Belgium

**Allons travailler! Waarom?
Waarom? Waarom?**
1991
single-channel video installation,
dimensions variable,
screen ratio 4:3
video transferred to DVD,
colour, stereo audio
38 min. 51 sec.
acquired directly from the artist
inv. no. K002785

JAN VERCRUYSSE
born in 1948 in Ostend, Belgium
lives in Brussels, Belgium

Labyrinth & Pleasure Gardens
conceived in 1994 – 95,
printed in 1995
portfolio, comprising eight
offset prints on paper, a title
and a colophon page, contained
in a cloth-covered folder
each sheet: 66 × 49 cm
this work is number sixty-five
from an edition of seventy-five
plus eight artist's proofs
published by Yves Gevaert,
Brussels
acquired directly from the artist
inv. no. K002789

Labyrinth & Pleasure Gardens
conceived in 1994 – 2001,
printed in 2002
portfolio, comprising thirteen
offset prints on paper, a title
and a colophon page
each sheet: 66 × 49 cm
this work is number thirty-seven
from an edition of forty-three
plus six artist's proofs and one
printer's proof
published by Brooke Alexander,
New York, Tucci Rosso, Torre
Pellice and Xavier Hufkens,
Brussels
acquired directly from the artist
inv. no. K002790

2009

Purchases

JEAN BRUSSELMANS
born in 1884 in Brussels, Belgium
died in 1953 in Dilbeek, Belgium

Au jardin
1916
pastel and ink and wash on paper
23 × 29.5 cm
acquired from a Belgian
private collector
inv. no. K002803(b)

[Cafe Scene]
n.d.
graphite on paper
22.5 × 23 cm
acquired from a Belgian
private collector
inv. no. K002810

[Cafe Scene]
n.d.
graphite on paper
24.5 × 25.5 cm
acquired from a Belgian
private collector
inv. no. K002805(b)

**[Composition with
Three Figures in a Triangle]**
ca. 1933
graphite on paper
24.5 × 25.5 cm
acquired from a Belgian
private collector
inv. no. K002805(a)

[Domestic Scene]
n.d.
graphite on paper
26.5 × 35.5 cm
acquired from a Belgian
private collector
inv. no. K002808(a)

[Exterior Scene with
Two Women and a Child]
n.d.
ink on paper
27 × 24 cm
acquired from a Belgian
private collector
inv. no. K002806(b)

[Farmers]
ca. 1928
graphite on paper
25.5 × 32 cm
acquired from a Belgian
private collector
inv. no. K002809(a)

[Farmers]
ca. 1928
graphite on paper
25.5 × 32 cm
acquired from a Belgian
private collector
inv. no. K002809(b)

[Farmers]
ca. 1928
graphite on paper
26.5 × 35.5 cm
acquired from a Belgian
private collector
inv. no. K002808(b)

Femme au chapeau
ca. 1914
charcoal on paper
27.5 × 19 cm
acquired from a Belgian
private collector
inv. no. K002802(a)

[Figure on a Canapé]
n.d.
graphite on paper
27.5 × 19 cm
acquired from a Belgian
private collector
inv. no. K002802(b)

[Figure Study]
n.d.
graphite on paper
22.5 × 12 cm
acquired from a Belgian

private collector
inv. no. K002807(b)

[Figure Study]
n.d.
watercolour, ink and wash
and graphite on paper
22.5 × 12 cm
acquired from a Belgian
private collector
inv. no. K002807(a)

[Houses]
n.d.
graphite on paper
18 × 14 cm
acquired from a Belgian
private collector
inv. no. K002792(b)

[Interior]
n.d.
ink on paper
23 × 29.5 cm
acquired from a Belgian
private collector
inv. no. K002803(a)

Kermesse
ca. 1930
graphite on paper
22.5 × 29.5 cm
acquired from a Belgian
private collector
inv. no. K002804(a)

Le patineur
ca. 1933
graphite on paper
29.5 × 23.5 cm
acquired from a Belgian
private collector
inv. no. K002804(b)

Ouvriers
ca. 1915
graphite on paper
14 × 18 cm
acquired from a Belgian
private collector
inv. no. K002792(a)

Reflet dans le miroir
[first of two states]
1915
etching on paper
sheet: 43.5 × 31 cm; image:
35.5 × 27 cm
acquired from a Belgian
private collector
inv. no. K002794(a)

Reflet dans le miroir
[second and final state]
1915
etching on paper
sheet: 38.5 × 32.5 cm; image:
32 × 28 cm
acquired from a Belgian
private collector
inv. no. K002794(b)

[Study of Heads]
n.d.
colour pencil on paper
27 × 24 cm
acquired from a Belgian
private collector
inv. no. K002806(a)

Tristesse
1927
charcoal on paper
27 × 20 cm
acquired from a Belgian
private collector
inv. no. K002793

LILI DUJOURIE
born in 1941 in Roeselare,
Belgium
lives in Lovendegem, Belgium

Il fait dimanche sur la mer
2009
seven-monitor video installation,
dimensions variable,
screen ratio 16:9
DVD, black and white,
stereo audio
each video: 24 hr.
this work is number one from
an edition of seven plus one
artist's proof
acquired from Ku(n)st vzw,

wooden structure: 108 × 45 × 73 cm
paint tin: 13.5 × 11 × 11 cm
acquired from De Notelaar nv,
Antwerp
inv. no. K002796

JAN VERCRUYSSE
born in 1948 in Ostend, Belgium
lives in Brussels, Belgium

L'Art de Voir, Les Choses
1977
silkscreen on paper, framed
print: 70 × 100 cm; incl. frame:
74 × 104 cm
acquired from R.D.W. nv,
Oostduinkerke
inv. no. K002799

Gifts

KOENRAAD DEDOBBELEER
born in 1975 in Halle, Belgium
lives in Brussels, Belgium

Cover Me Slowly
2009
six elements – latex paint on
wood blocks
overall: ca. 61 × 95 × 61 cm
element i: 61 × 22 × 11.5 cm
element ii: 39 × 19.5 × 11 cm
element iii: 28 × 20 × 11 cm
element iv: 23 × 22 × 11.5 cm
element v: 20 × 35 × 21 cm
element vi: 20 × 30 × 11 cm
gift from the artist
inv. no. K002801

VALÉRIE MANNAERTS
born in 1974 in Brussels,
Belgium
lives in Brussels, Belgium

**If travel is searching and home
what's been found (yellow dots)**
2009

concrete, silicate paint in
Le Corbusier colours
140 × 60 × 60 cm
gift from the artist
inv. no. K002791(a)

**If travel is searching and home
what's been found (bow tie with
pink body)**
2009
concrete, silicate paint in
Le Corbusier colours
118 × 60 × 60 cm
gift from the artist
inv. no. K002791(b)

**If travel is searching and home
what's been found (pink bow
tie)**
2009
concrete, silicate paint in
Le Corbusier colours
115 × 40 × 30 cm
gift from the artist
inv. no. K002791(c)

**If travel is searching and home
what's been found (napkin)**
2009
concrete, silicate paint in
Le Corbusier colours
40 × 20 × 20 cm
gift from the artist
inv. no. K002791(d)

2010

Purchases

ABEL AUER
born in 1974 in Munich, Germany
lives in Brussels, Belgium

The Message
2010
acrylic and oil on canvas
200 × 210 cm
acquired from Corvi-Mora,
London
inv. no. MZ000004

JEAN BRUSSELMANS
born in 1884 in Brussels, Belgium
died in 1953 in Dilbeek, Belgium

[Barge]
ca. 1947
crayon on paper
36 × 27 cm
acquired from International
Consulting Services nv, Deinze
inv. no. MZ000022

[Barges]
ca. 1947
graphite on paper
27 × 36 cm
acquired from International
Consulting Services nv, Deinze
inv. no. MZ000033(a)

**Bataille de gamins dans une
rue de Paris**
1949–50
ink on paper
30 × 27 cm
acquired from International
Consulting Services nv, Deinze
inv. no. MZ000017

Consulting Services nv, Deinze
inv. no. MZ000019

[On the Dry Dock]
ca. 1952
crayon on paper
27 × 36 cm
acquired from International
Consulting Services nv, Deinze
inv. no. MZ000023

[Outport]
ca. 1947
graphite on paper
28 × 36 cm
acquired from International
Consulting Services nv, Deinze
inv. no. MZ000015(a)

[Palisade]
1952
crayon on paper
27 × 36 cm
acquired from International
Consulting Services nv, Deinze
inv. no. MZ000020

[Palisade and Dunes]
1952
crayon on paper
27 × 36 cm
acquired from International
Consulting Services nv, Deinze
inv. no. MZ000021

[Party in the Harbour]
ca. 1949
crayon on paper
26.5 × 35.5 cm
acquired from International
Consulting Services nv, Deinze
inv. no. MZ000028

Portrait de René Lyr
1915
ink on paper
61 × 39 cm
acquired from International
Consulting Services nv, Deinze
inv. no. MZ000030

[Pub]
n.d.
graphite on paper

27.5 × 36.5 cm
acquired from International
Consulting Services nv, Deinze
inv. no. MZ000034(a)

[Sailors by a Boat]
ca. 1947
graphite on paper
36 × 28 cm
acquired from International
Consulting Services nv, Deinze
inv. no. MZ000015(b)

[Studies for Le pont]
ca. 1930
graphite on paper
38 × 25 cm
acquired from International
Consulting Services nv, Deinze
inv. no. MZ000036(b)

[Study for a Still Life]
1938
graphite on paper
27.5 × 36.5 cm
acquired from International
Consulting Services nv, Deinze
inv. no. MZ000034(b)

[Study for L'élagueur]
ca. 1930
graphite on paper
36 × 27 cm
acquired from International
Consulting Services nv, Deinze
inv. no. MZ000014(a)

[Study for Le pont]
1930
graphite on paper
27 × 36 cm
acquired from International
Consulting Services nv, Deinze
inv. no. MZ000036(a)

[Study for Le pont]
ca. 1930
graphite on paper
38 × 25 cm
acquired from International
Consulting Services nv, Deinze
inv. no. MZ000046

[Various Interior Scenes]
ca. 1938
graphite on paper
26 × 36 cm
acquired from International
Consulting Services nv, Deinze
inv. no. MZ000031(a)

[Workers in the Field]
n.d.
graphite on paper
26 × 37.5 cm
acquired from International
Consulting Services nv, Deinze
inv. no. MZ000035(b)

ANNE DAEMS
born in 1966 in Lier, Belgium
lives in Brussels, Belgium

My Father's Garden
2008
six-monitor video installation,
dimensions variable,
screen ratio 4:3
DVD, colour, stereo audio
video i (two chapters):
9 min. 59 sec.
video ii (one chapter):
7 min. 25 sec.
video iii (two chapters):
11 min. 49 sec.
video iv (one chapter):
5 min. 44 sec.
video v (one chapter):
4 min. 14 sec.
video vi (one chapter):
3 min. 46 sec.
this work is number two from
an edition of three plus one
artist's proof
acquired from Elisa Platteau
Galerie, Brussels
inv. no. K002797

BERT DE BEUL
born in 1961 in Ghent, Belgium
lives in Antwerp, Belgium

Untitled
2000
oil on canvas

cotton, painted wooden
pedestal, rollers, rail, metal
hooks
380 × 1250 × 244 cm
acquired directly from the artist
inv. no. MZ000005

WALTER SWENNEN
born in 1946 in Vorst, Belgium
lives in Brussels, Belgium

Untitled
2010
oil on canvas
150 × 135 cm
acquired from Aliceday, Brussels
inv. no. MZ000037

MICHAEL VAN DEN ABEELE
born in 1974 in Brussels,
Belgium
lives in Brussels, Belgium

Blauwe Blisters
2010
oil on canvas
123 × 85 cm
acquired from Elisa Platteau
Galerie, Brussels
inv. no. MZ000038

Sleeper Service
2010
oil on canvas
120.5 × 87 cm
acquired from Elisa Platteau
Galerie, Brussels
inv. no. MZ000039

JAN VERCRUYSSE
born in 1948 in Ostend, Belgium
lives in Brussels, Belgium

Zonder Titel (Zelfportretten) IX
1980
three photolithoprints on paper,
individually framed
overall: ca. 69 × 92 cm
print i, incl. frame: 52 × 48.5 cm
print ii, incl. frame: 37 × 37 cm
print iii, incl. frame: 25 × 31.5 cm

acquired from a Belgian
private collector
inv. no. MZ000002

Gifts

PHILIP AGUIRRE Y OTEGUI
born in 1961 in Schoten, Belgium
lives in Antwerp, Belgium

**Untitled [from the series
Édition populaire]**
2010
woodcut on paper
sheet: 33 × 46 cm; image:
10 × 20.5 cm
this work is the artist's proof
from an edition of thirty plus
one artist's proof
gift from the artist
inv. no. MZ000042(a)

**Untitled [from the series
Édition populaire]**
2010
woodcut on paper
sheet: 33 × 46 cm; image:
21 × 30 cm
this work is the artist's proof
from an edition of thirty plus
one artist's proof
gift from the artist
inv. no. MZ000042(b)

**Untitled [from the series
Édition populaire]**
2010
woodcut on paper
sheet: 33 × 46 cm; image:
21 × 30 cm
this work is the artist's proof
from an edition of thirty plus
one artist's proof
gift from the artist
inv. no. MZ000042(c)

**Untitled [from the series
Édition populaire]**
2010

woodcut on paper
sheet: 46 × 33 cm; image:
12 × 20 cm
this work is the artist's proof
from an edition of thirty plus
one artist's proof
gift from the artist
inv. no. MZ000042(d)

**Untitled [from the series
Édition populaire]**
2010
woodcut on paper
sheet: 46 × 33 cm; image:
15 × 9.5 cm
this work is the artist's proof
from an edition of thirty plus
one artist's proof
gift from the artist
inv. no. MZ000042(e)

**Untitled [from the series
Édition populaire]**
2010
colour woodcut on paper
sheet: 46 × 33 cm; image:
19.5 × 11.5 cm
this work is the artist's proof
from an edition of thirty plus
one artist's proof
gift from the artist
inv. no. MZ000042(f)

**Untitled [from the series
Édition populaire]**
2010
woodcut on paper
sheet: 46 × 33 cm; image:
20.5 × 14.5 cm
this work is the artist's proof
from an edition of thirty plus
one artist's proof
gift from the artist
inv. no. MZ000042(g)

**Untitled [from the series
Édition populaire]**
2010
colour woodcut on paper
sheet: 46 × 33 cm; image:
21 × 15 cm
this work is the artist's proof
from an edition of thirty plus
one artist's proof

gift from the artist
inv. no. MZ000042(h)

**Untitled [from the series
Édition populaire]**
2010
woodcut on paper
sheet: 46 × 33 cm; image:
21 × 15 cm
this work is the artist's proof
from an edition of thirty plus
one artist's proof
gift from the artist
inv. no. MZ000042(i)

**Untitled [from the series
Édition populaire]**
2010
woodcut on paper
sheet: 46 × 33 cm; image:
23.5 × 16 cm
this work is the artist's proof
from an edition of thirty plus
one artist's proof
gift from the artist
inv. no. MZ000042(j)

**Untitled [from the series
Édition populaire]**
2010
woodcut on paper
sheet: 46 × 33 cm; image:
28.5 × 18 cm
this work is the artist's proof
from an edition of thirty plus
one artist's proof
gift from the artist
inv. no. MZ000042(k)

**Untitled [from the series
Édition populaire]**
2010
woodcut on paper
sheet: 46 × 33 cm; image:
30 × 21 cm
this work is the artist's proof
from an edition of thirty plus
one artist's proof
gift from the artist
inv. no. MZ000042(l)

**Untitled [from the series
Édition populaire]**
2010

woodcut on paper
sheet: 46 × 33 cm; image:
30 × 21 cm
this work is the artist's proof
from an edition of thirty plus
one artist's proof
gift from the artist
inv. no. MZ000042(m)

**Untitled [from the series
Édition populaire]**
2010
woodcut on paper
sheet: 46 × 33 cm; image:
30 × 21 cm
this work is the artist's proof
from an edition of thirty plus
one artist's proof
gift from the artist
inv. no. MZ000042(n)

LUC CLAUS
born in 1930 in Aalst, Belgium
died in 2006 in Brussels,
Belgium

**[Study for the Décor Design
of the Ballet Pantomime
'Masques ostendais']**
1965
watercolour and ink on paper
27 × 36.5 cm
gift from Dirk Claeys
inv. no. MZ000045

RONNY DELRUE
born in 1957 in Heestert,
Belgium
lives in Ghent, Belgium

[Study for Vive la liberté d'art art]
2010
ink on paper
29.5 × 21 cm
gift from the artist
inv. no. MZ000161

HELMUT STALLAERTS
born in 1982 in Brussels, Belgium
lives in Lennik, Belgium

The Fog
2010
oil and ink on textile
198 × 101 cm
gift from the artist
inv. no. MZ000040

ANNE-MIE VAN KERCKHOVEN
born in 1951 in Antwerp, Belgium
lives in Antwerp, Belgium

**À la Globalité [from the series
Zeven Keer Vallen per Dag]**
2005
watercolour, pastel and ink
on paper
29.5 × 42 cm
gift from De Vrienden van
Mu.ZEE, collectie Provincie
West-Vlaanderen vzw, Ostend
inv. no. MZ000043(i)

**Autre Chose [from the series
Zeven Keer Vallen per Dag]**
2005
pastel, ink and paper collage
on paper
29.5 × 42 cm
gift from De Vrienden van
Mu.ZEE, collectie Provincie
West-Vlaanderen vzw, Ostend
inv. no. MZ000043(d)

**De l'Aide [from the series
Zeven Keer Vallen per Dag]**
2005
watercolour, pastel and ink
on paper
29.5 × 42 cm
gift from De Vrienden van
Mu.ZEE, collectie Provincie
West-Vlaanderen vzw, Ostend
inv. no. MZ000043(b)

**En Zo de Wolken Lomp Zweten,
Zo Maakt Gij Mij Bang
[from the series Zeven Keer
Vallen per Dag]**
2005
pastel and ink on paper
29.5 × 42 cm
gift from De Vrienden van
Mu.ZEE, collectie Provincie

West-Vlaanderen vzw, Ostend
inv. no. MZ000043(g)

**Fluide Humain [from the series
Zeven Keer Vallen per Dag]**
2005
pastel, ink and coloured pencil
on paper
29.5 × 42 cm
gift from De Vrienden van
Mu.ZEE, collectie Provincie
West-Vlaanderen vzw, Ostend
inv. no. MZ000043(h)

**In Zwarte Bastarda
[from the series Zeven Keer
Vallen per Dag]**
2005
pastel, ink, coloured pencil and
paper collage on paper
29.5 × 42 cm
gift from De Vrienden van
Mu.ZEE, collectie Provincie
West-Vlaanderen vzw, Ostend
inv. no. MZ000043(e)

**L'Aimant [from the series
Zeven Keer Vallen per Dag]**
2005
watercolour, pastel and ink
on paper
29.5 × 42 cm
gift from De Vrienden van
Mu.ZEE, collectie Provincie
West-Vlaanderen vzw, Ostend
inv. no. MZ000043(c)

**L'Âme et Ses Demandes
[from the series Zeven Keer
Vallen per Dag]**
2005
pastel, ink and paper collage
on paper
29.5 × 42 cm
gift from De Vrienden van
Mu.ZEE, collectie Provincie
West-Vlaanderen vzw, Ostend
inv. no. MZ000043(j)

**Le Juste Tombe 7 Fois par Jour
[from the series Zeven Keer
Vallen per Dag]**
2005
pastel, coloured pencil and ink

on paper
29.5 × 42 cm
gift from De Vrienden van
Mu.ZEE, collectie Provincie
West-Vlaanderen vzw, Ostend
inv. no. MZ000043(k)

**Une Chambre Noire
[from the series Zeven Keer
Vallen per Dag]**
2005
pastel, coloured pencil and ink
on paper
29.5 × 42 cm
gift from De Vrienden van
Mu.ZEE, collectie Provincie
West-Vlaanderen vzw, Ostend
inv. no. MZ000043(a)

**Van Ver en Lang Geleden
[from the series Zeven Keer
Vallen per Dag]**
2005
pastel and ink on paper
29.5 × 42 cm
gift from De Vrienden van
Mu.ZEE, collectie Provincie
West-Vlaanderen vzw, Ostend
inv. no. MZ000043(f)

**Wie Durft nog Beweren te Zijn
Verrast als Zij Getweeën
Zonder Zon Zonder Kleren
Vermorzeld Gevonden Zijn
Dood door Innig Verstrelen
[from the series Zeven Keer
Vallen per Dag]**
2005
watercolour, pastel, ink and
paper collage on paper
29.5 × 42 cm
gift from De Vrienden van
Mu.ZEE, collectie Provincie
West-Vlaanderen vzw, Ostend
inv. no. MZ000043(l)

YVES VELTER
born in 1967 in Ostend, Belgium
lives in Ostend, Belgium

Floating
2010
mixed media – bronze, paint,

multiplex, MDF and metal
154 × 40.5 × 36.5 cm
gift from Vrienden Mu.ZEE
Oostende, collectie van de stad
Oostende vzw, Ostend
inv. no. MZ000041

VADIM VOSTERS
born in 1979 in Colmar, France
lives in Brussels, Belgium

V.V.
2010
acrylic on textile
149 × 142 cm
gift from the artist
inv. no. MZ000162

VARIOUS ARTISTS

**[20th Anniversary Portfolio De
Vrienden van Mu.ZEE, collectie
Provincie West-Vlaanderen vzw]**
2009 – 10
portfolio, comprising five sheets
– prints on paper by Louis De
Cordier, Joris Ghekiere,
Catharina Van Eetvelde, Yves
Velter and Pieter Vermeersch
all: 42 × 30 or 30 × 42 cm
this work is from an edition of
one hundred
published by De Vrienden van
Mu.ZEE, collectie Provincie
West-Vlaanderen vzw, Ostend
gift from De Vrienden van
Mu.ZEE, collectie Provincie
West-Vlaanderen vzw, Ostend
inv. no. MZ000061 – 65

2011

Purchases

SVEN AUGUSTIJNEN
born in 1970 in Mechelen,
Belgium
lives in Brussels, Belgium

Spectres
2011
single-screen video projection,
dimensions variable,
screen ratio 16:9
DVD, colour, stereo audio
1 hr. 43 min. 8 sec.
this work is number one from
an edition of three plus one
artist's proof
acquired from Projections vzw,
Brussels
inv. no. MZ000067

JEAN BRUSSELMANS
born in 1884 in Brussels, Belgium
died in 1953 in Dilbeek, Belgium

Arc-en-ciel en mer
conceived ca. 1920, printed
in 1982
engraving on paper
sheet: 37 × 57 cm; image:
17 × 20 cm
this work is number eight
from an edition of twenty-five
plus an unknown number of
artist's proofs
acquired from XXL ART on
Waterloo 503, Brussels
inv. no. MZ000048

Autoportrait
conceived ca. 1920, printed
in 1982
engraving on paper
sheet: 57 × 37.5 cm; image:
19.5 × 17 cm
this work is number seven

from an edition of twenty-five
plus an unknown number of
artist's proofs
acquired from XXL ART on
Waterloo 503, Brussels
inv. no. MZ000049

Autoportrait à la pipe
conceived in 1915, printed
in 1982
engraving on paper
sheet: 57 × 38 cm; image:
17.5 × 14 cm
this work is number four
from an edition of twenty-five
plus an unknown number of
artist's proofs
acquired from XXL ART on
Waterloo 503, Brussels
inv. no. MZ000047

Autoportrait au Paruck
conceived in 1920, printed
in 1982
woodcut on paper
sheet: 60.5 × 40 cm; image:
23 × 26.5 cm
this work is number nine
from an edition of twenty-five
plus an unknown number of
artist's proofs
acquired from XXL ART on
Waterloo 503, Brussels
inv. no. MZ000051

Baigneuse
conceived in 1934, printed
in 1982
engraving on paper
sheet: 57 × 37 cm; image:
36.5 × 17 cm
this work is number eight
from an edition of twenty-five
plus an unknown number of
artist's proofs
acquired from XXL ART on
Waterloo 503, Brussels
inv. no. MZ000053

Le gâcheur de plâtre
conceived in 1924, printed
in 1982
engraving on paper
sheet: 56.5 × 38 cm; image:

21.5 × 19.5 cm
this work is number thirteen
from an edition of twenty-five
plus an unknown number of
artist's proofs
acquired from XXL ART on
Waterloo 503, Brussels
inv. no. MZ000050

Nature morte au griffon
1936
oil on canvas
109.5 × 122.5 cm
acquired from Keitelman Gallery,
Brussels
inv. no. MZ000054

Ouvriers au canal
conceived in 1920, printed
in 1982
woodcut on paper
sheet: 63 × 40 cm; image:
22.5 × 25.5 cm
this work is number eleven
from an edition of twenty-five
plus an unknown number of
artist's proofs
acquired from XXL ART on
Waterloo 503, Brussels
inv. no. MZ000052

KOENRAAD DEDOBBELEER
born in 1975 in Halle, Belgium
lives in Brussels, Belgium

Organogramme
2011
mixed media – i.a. wood, metal,
paint, melaminated chipboard
and an orchid
ca. 130 × 75 × 75 cm
acquired from Galerie Micheline
Szwajcer, Antwerp
inv. no. MZ000079

Theoretical Length
2011
mixed media – wood, metal,
paint
76.5 × 33 × 29 cm
acquired from Galerie Micheline
Szwajcer, Antwerp
inv. no. MZ000080

**JOS DE GRUYTER &
HARALD THYS**
born in 1965 in Geel, Belgium
born in 1966, Wilrijk, Belgium
live in Brussels, Belgium

Johannes, painter, *1947 †2010
2011
mixed media – wood, metal
and various materials in a
plexiglass vitrine on a painted
wooden socle
95 × 238 × 88 cm
acquired from Galerie Micheline
Szwajcer, Antwerp
inv. no. MZ000078

Untitled
2010
178 C-prints mounted on wood
each: 48 × 60 cm
acquired from Isabella Bortolozzi
Galerie, Berlin
inv. no. MZ000068

LILI DUJOURIE
born in 1941 in Roeselare, Belgium
lives in Lovendegem, Belgium

Crépuscule
1985
mixed media – wood, paint and
textile
299.5 × 246.5 × 143 cm
acquired from a Belgian private
collector
inv. no. MZ000071

PIETERJAN GINCKELS
born in 1982 in Tienen, Belgium
lives in Brussels, Belgium

1000 Beats
2008
a variable number of turntables,
amplifiers, mix panels,
loudspeakers and 7-inch
vinyl records *One Beat*
(sleeve and label design by
Grandpeople, music by
Cristian Vogel)
dimensions variable

acquired from Galerie
de Expeditie, Amsterdam
inv. no. MZ000075

DOROTA JURCZAK
born in 1978 in Warsaw, Poland
lives in Brussels, Belgium

Laski
2011
acrylic, ink and paper on wood
90 × 11 × 0.5 cm
this work is from an edition of
four unique pieces
acquired from Der Kunstverein,
seit 1817, Hamburg
inv. no. MZ000082

Mimosa
2010
vinyl paint and ink on canvas
60 × 50 cm
acquired from Corvi-Mora,
London
inv. no. MZ000066

AGLAIA KONRAD
born in 1960 in Salzburg, Austria
lives in Brussels, Belgium

Carrara (Blocs 1 – 14)
2010
fourteen black and white photos –
digital print on aluminum
each sheet: 30.5 × 21 cm; each
image: 28.5 × 19 cm
this work is number one from
an edition of three plus one
artist's proof
acquired from Galerie Nadja
Vilenne, Liège
inv. no. MZ000060

Carrara (Mountains 1 – 8)
2010
eight colour photos – archival
pigment print on paper
each: 77 × 55 cm
this work is number one from
an edition of three plus one
artist's proof
acquired from Galerie Nadja

Vilenne, Liège
inv. no. MZ000069

VALÉRIE MANNAERTS
born in 1974 in Brussels, Belgium
lives in Brussels, Belgium

Diamond Dancer (paravent)
2010
showcase with pedestal in
painted wood and glass;
wooden screen with drawings in
oil pastel, pastel and pencil
240 × 240 × 105 cm
acquired from Elisa Platteau
& Cie Galerie, Brussels
inv. no. MZ000076

MARC NAGTZAAM
born in 1968 in Helmond,
the Netherlands
lives in Antwerp, Belgium

Lines (Versions)
2004
graphite on paper
71 × 55.5 cm
acquired from ProjecteSD,
Barcelona
inv. no. MZ000072

Show (Antwerp, 1999)
2000
five drawings – graphite on paper
each: 28.5 × 43 cm
acquired from ProjecteSD,
Barcelona
inv. no. MZ000073

Slightly All the Time
2005
graphite on paper
68 × 56 cm
acquired from ProjecteSD,
Barcelona
inv. no. MZ000074

MICHAEL VAN DEN ABEELE
born in 1974 in Brussels, Belgium
lives in Brussels, Belgium

Nuit de Plomb
2011
oil on canvas
116.5 × 87 cm
acquired from Elisa Platteau
& Cie Galerie, Brussels
inv. no. MZ000081

PHILIPPE VAN SNICK
born in 1946 in Ghent, Belgium
lives in Brussels, Belgium

Perspectieven I
2004
acrylic on canvas
38.5 × 45.5 cm
acquired directly from the artist
inv. no. MZ000056

Perspectieven II
2004
acrylic on canvas
32.5 × 42 cm
acquired directly from the artist
inv. no. MZ000057

Perspectieven III
2004
acrylic and cut on canvas
41 × 47.5 cm
acquired directly from the artist
inv. no. MZ000058

Perspectieven IV
2004
acrylic on canvas
42 × 48.5 cm
acquired directly from the artist
inv. no. MZ000059

GEORGES VANTONGERLOO
born in 1886 in Antwerp,
Belgium
died in 1965 in Paris, France

Autoportrait
1916
oil on canvas
100 × 75 cm
acquired from Kunstsalon
Franke-Schenk, Munich
inv. no. MZ000070

ISIDORE VERHEYDEN
born in 1846 in Antwerp, Belgium
died in 1907 in Ixelles, Belgium

[Portrait of the Printer Léon Evely]
1890
oil on canvas
147 × 92 cm
acquired from Patrick Florizoone
inv. no. MZ000160

VARIOUS ARTISTS

Das Mappenwerk der Insel
1900
portfolio comprising forty sheets
– twenty-four original prints on
paper by Anton Albers, Paul
Baum, Pierre Bonnard, Frank
Brangwyn, Eugène Delâtre,
Maurice Denis, James Ensor,
Ernst Moritz Geyger, Henri-
Gabriel Ibels, Wilhelm Laage,
Georges Lemmen, Max
Liebermann, William Nicholson,
Auguste Rodin, Max Stremel,
Hans Thoma, Heinrich Vogeler,
Édouard Vuillard, Emil Rudolf
Weiss and Ignacio Zuloaga;
sixteen facsimile reproductions
on paper of works by Max
Dauthendey, Eugène Delacroix,
Albrecht Dürer, Constant Guys,
Utagawa Kunisada II, Édouard
Manet, Okumura Massanobu,
Pisanello, Giovanni Batista
Scultori, Utagawa Toyohiro, Jan
Van Eyck and several
anonymous masters – in a
cardboard folder with vellum
spine
sheets: various sizes (mostly:
35.5 × 27.5 cm)
this work is from an edition of
one hundred
edited by Otto Julius Bierbaum,
Alfred Walter Heymel and
Rudolf Alexander Schröder
published by Insel-Verlag,
Leipzig
acquired from Patrick Florizoone
inv. no. MZ000083

Gifts

VALÉRIE MANNAERTS
born in 1974 in Brussels,
Belgium
lives in Brussels, Belgium

Geometrical Fantasy
2010
wool, pencil and nine metal rings
on cotton
187.5 × 262 cm
gift from the artist
inv. no. MZ000077

VARIOUS ARTISTS

Re:print
2009
portfolio of six sheets –
prints on paper by Ronny Delrue,
Honoré d'O, Kendell Geers,
Vincent Geyskens, Tina Gillen
and Pieter Vermeersch –
in a cardboard folder
each sheet: 76.5 × 56 cm or
56 × 76.5 cm
this portfolio is number twelve
from an edition of twenty
published by Frans Masereel
Centrum, Kasterlee
gift from Frans Masereel
Centrum, Kasterlee
inv. no. MZ000044

2012

Purchases

ABEL AUER
born in 1974 in Munich, Germany
lives in Brussels, Belgium

Protection and Punishment
2010
acrylic, oil and ink on canvas
174.5 × 240.5 cm
acquired from Corvi-Mora,
London
inv. no. MZ000120

KOENRAAD DEDOBBELEER
born in 1975 in Halle, Belgium
lives in Brussels, Belgium

An Object of Disdain
2012
pigment print on paper, framed
print: 39.5 × 30 cm; incl. frame:
41 × 31 cm
this work is number one from an
open edition of unique pieces
acquired from Reception, Berlin
inv. no. MZ000154

Stragglers and Laggards
2011
mixed media – enamel paint,
varnish, wood, copper, metal,
resin, plastic and part of a
coconut shell
124 × 63 × 61.5 cm
acquired from Mai 36 Galerie,
Zurich
inv. no. MZ000155

**JOS DE GRUYTER &
HARALD THYS**
born in 1965 in Geel, Belgium
born in 1966 in Wilrijk, Belgium
live in Brussels, Belgium

Untitled
2010 – 11
128 C-prints mounted on wood
each: 48 × 60 cm
acquired from Isabella Bortolozzi
Galerie, Berlin
inv. no. MZ000068

PETER DOWNSBROUGH
born in 1940 in New Brunswick,
United States
lives in Brussels, Belgium

Rotterdam
1992
ten gelatin silver prints on paper,
matted, in a linen-covered box
each print: 24 × 30 cm
this work is number nineteen
from an edition of twenty plus
five artist's proofs
published by The Archives,
Rotterdam
acquired from Thomas Zander
Galerie, Cologne
inv. no. MZ000121

JEF GEYS
born in 1934 in Leopoldsburg,
Belgium
lives in Balen, Belgium

Gypsophila Elegans
2008
oil on canvas
canvas: 26 × 16.5 cm
acquired from Galerie Greta
Meert, Brussels
inv. no. MZ000124

Gypsophila Elegans
2008
three elements –
(i) mixed media on melaminated
chipboard – i.a. chalk paint,
lacquer, pastel and ink
(ii) digital print on paper, framed
(iii) digital print on paper, framed
overall: 215 × 90 cm
(i) 140 × 90 cm
(ii) incl. frame: 22.5 × 90 cm
(iii) incl. frame: 13 × 27 cm

acquired from Galerie Greta
Meert, Brussels
inv. no. MZ000125

GABRIEL KURI
born in 1970 in Mexico City,
Mexico
lives in Brussels, Belgium

Flat Hole
2012
digital print on fabric, hung on
a perforated wall
overall: dimensions variable;
fabric: 400 × 600 cm
acquired from Kurimanzutto,
Mexico City
inv. no. MZ000115

LUCY MCKENZIE
born in 1977 in Glasgow,
United Kingdom
lives in Brussels, Belgium

Stoffenverkoop
2012
oil on canvas
280 × 460 cm
acquired from Galerie Buchholz,
Berlin / Cologne
inv. no. MZ000105

JOE SCANLAN
born in 1961 in Stoutsville,
United States
lives in New York City,
United States

Nesting Bookcases
2012
twenty bookcases and two
prototypes of these bookcases
mixed media – wood, paint
and plastic
each: dimensions variable
(min: 44 × 79 × 22 cm)
acquired directly from the artist
inv. no. MZ000122

Turning Mountains into Sea
[from the series Sisyphus,
gelukkig]
2010
mixed media on paper –
i.a. pastel, ink and collage
31 × 30 cm
acquired from Zeno X Gallery,
Antwerp
inv. no. MZ000097

PHILIPPE VAN SNICK
born in 1946 in Ghent, Belgium
lives in Brussels, Belgium

The Archive Revisited: Iris Pond
Botanical Garden, Osaka Japan
1995 / 2012
acrylic on a digital print on paper,
framed
print: 65 × 95 cm; incl. frame:
75 × 105 cm
acquired directly from the artist
inv. no. MZ000156

The Archive Revisited: Wall,
Osaka Japan
1995 / 2012
acrylic on a digital print on paper,
framed
print: 65 × 95 cm; incl. frame:
75 × 105 cm
acquired directly from the artist
inv. no. MZ000157

GEORGES VANTONGERLOO
born in 1886 in Antwerp, Belgium
died in 1965 in Paris, France

[Figure Study]
1914
watercolour on paper
39 × 49 cm
acquired from a private collector
inv. no. MZ000119

[Figure Study]
ca. 1915
charcoal and paint on paper
65 × 51 cm
acquired from a private collector
inv. no. MZ000118

JULIE VAN WEZEMAEL
born in 1990 in Ostend, Belgium
lives in Ostend, Belgium

Museumzicht
2012
mixed media on paper –
i.a. acrylic, dry-point, graphite
and textile embroidery
42 × 59.5 cm
gift from JCI Oostende, Ostend
inv. no. MZ000114

JAN VERCRUYSSE
born in 1948 in Ostend, Belgium
lives in Brussels, Belgium

De L'Art
conceived in 2004, printed
in 2011
digital print on paper, framed
print: 42 × 29.5 cm; incl. frame:
48.5 × 36 cm
this work is number one from an
edition of fifteen plus three
artist's proofs
acquired from Xavier Hufkens,
Brussels
inv. no. MZ000087

Goethe in Italy
conceived in 2009, printed
in 2011
digital print on paper, framed
print: 33 × 48.5 cm; incl. frame:
43 × 57.5 cm
this work is number one from an
edition of fifteen plus three
artist's proofs
acquired from Xavier Hufkens,
Brussels
inv. no. MZ000089

Les Consonants
conceived in 2010, printed
in 2011
digital print on paper, framed
print: 59.5 × 42 cm; incl. frame:
67.5 × 49.5 cm
this work is number two from an
edition of fifteen plus three
artist's proofs
acquired from Xavier Hufkens,

Brussels
inv. no. MZ000090

Mille Illusionen
conceived in 2006, printed
in 2011
digital print on paper, framed
print: 42 × 59.5 cm; incl. frame:
50.5 × 67.5 cm
this work is number two from an
edition of fifteen plus three
artist's proofs
acquired from Xavier Hufkens,
Brussels
inv. no. MZ000088

Revolution
conceived in 2002, printed
in 2011
digital print on paper, framed
print: 33 × 48.5 cm; incl. frame:
43 × 57.5 cm
this work is number one from an
edition of fifteen plus three
artist's proofs
acquired from Xavier Hufkens,
Brussels
inv. no. MZ000086

Schneckengang (1)
conceived in 2010, printed
in 2011
digital print on paper, framed
print: 42 × 59.5 cm; incl. frame:
50.5 × 67.5 cm
this work is number one from an
edition of fifteen plus three
artist's proofs
acquired from Xavier Hufkens,
Brussels
inv. no. MZ000091

Schneckengang (2)
conceived in 2010, printed
in 2011
digital print on paper, framed
print: 33 × 48.5 cm; incl. frame:
43 × 57.5 cm
this work is number one from an
edition of fifteen plus three
artist's proofs
acquired from Xavier Hufkens,
Brussels
inv. no. MZ000092

oil paint and ink on a ceramic tile
10 × 10 × 1 cm
gift from Jozef Gijsbrechts
inv. no. MZ000146

**[Painted Tile, to Be Looked at
from All Angles]**
1943
oil paint and ink on a ceramic tile
10 × 10 × 1 cm
gift from Jozef Gijsbrechts
inv. no. MZ000147

**[Painted Tile, to Be Looked at
from All Angles]**
1943
oil paint on wood
16.5 × 16.5 × 0.5 cm
gift from Jozef Gijsbrechts
inv. no. MZ000144

[Proof for Wallpaper U.P.L.]
1922
print on paper
31 × 49 cm
gift from Jozef Gijsbrechts
inv. no. MZ000134

[Proof for Wallpaper U.P.L.]
1922
print on paper
57 × 49 cm
gift from Jozef Gijsbrechts
inv. no. MZ000140

[Proof for Wallpaper U.P.L.]
1922
print on paper
64 × 47 cm
gift from Jozef Gijsbrechts
inv. no. MZ000137

[Proof for Wallpaper U.P.L.]
ca. 1920–25
print on paper
62 × 47.5 cm
gift from Jozef Gijsbrechts
inv. no. MZ000136

**[Proof for Wallpaper
U.P.L. 14469]**
1921
print on paper
68 × 47.5 cm

gift from Jozef Gijsbrechts
inv. no. MZ000141

**[Proof for Wallpaper
U.P.L. 14551]**
1921
print on paper
71 × 50 cm
gift from Jozef Gijsbrechts
inv. no. MZ000135

**[Proof for Wallpaper
U.P.L. 14731]**
1923
print on paper
59 × 47 cm
gift from Jozef Gijsbrechts
inv. no. MZ000139

**[Proof for Wallpaper
U.P.L. 5477 H2]**
1925
print on paper
31 × 48 cm
gift from Jozef Gijsbrechts
inv. no. MZ000133

**[Proof for Wallpaper
U.P.L. M 14800 H6]**
1922
print on paper
30 × 38 cm
gift from Jozef Gijsbrechts
inv. no. MZ000127

**[Proof for Wallpaper
U.P.L. M 14990 H2]**
1923
print on paper
48 × 37 cm
gift from Jozef Gijsbrechts
inv. no. MZ000128

**[Proof for Wallpaper
U.P.L. MA 14736]**
1924
print on paper
76 × 54.5 cm
gift from Jozef Gijsbrechts
inv. no. MZ000143

**[Rose. Design for
Wallpaper U.P.L.]**
1922

gouache on paper
47 × 31 cm
gift from Jozef Gijsbrechts
inv. no. MZ000129

**[Study for Opus 56 – 1921
(Pont dans le brouillard)]**
1920
charcoal and graphite on paper
33 × 43 cm
gift from Jozef Gijsbrechts
inv. no. MZ00084

**[The Parrots. Proof for
Wallpaper U.P.L. M 14800 H6]**
1922
print on paper
30 × 38 cm
gift from Jozef Gijsbrechts
inv. no. MZ000131

**[The Parrots. Proof for
Wallpaper U.P.L. M 4800 H2]**
1922
print on paper
30 × 40 cm
gift from Jozef Gijsbrechts
inv. no. MZ000132

PETER VAN AMMEL
born in 1976 in Wilrijk, Belgium
lives in Kortrijk, Belgium

**Trompe l'art, trompe
la mort**
2012
oil on canvas
150 × 170 cm
gift from Comitee Mu.ZEE,
Ostend
inv. no. MZ000152

ROBIN VANBESIEN
born in 1979 in Ostend, Belgium
lives in Brussels, Belgium

**A Figure Hovering above
the Carpet**
2011
pastel and dye on textile on
a wooden stretcher
105 × 100 × 2 cm

Colophon

With the support of

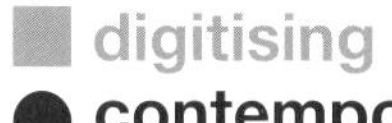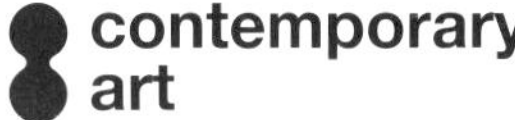

digitising contemporary art

Digitising Contemporary Art is a 30-month digiti-sation project for contemporary art, i.e. art made after 1945 – a type of cultural heritage still largely missing in Europeana. It comprises paintings, photo-graphs, sculptures, installations, videos… DCA creates a digital corpus of high-quality reproductions of 26,921 artworks and 1,857 contextual documents, and makes it accessible and retrievable through Europeana; not only metadata and thumbnails, but also direct links to large-sized reproductions of each item. DCA assures that the rights on all available digital content are cleared. The supplied content, including masterpieces from key artists of most European countries, fills a gap in Europeana's content supply.
The main issues of the project are the choice of specifications for digitisation and metadata, in order to make them interoperable, and finding the appropriate aggregation solution for each institution. The exchange with Europeana is the major result of the project. DCA's digitisation action also contri-butes to the preservation of the artworks.

This book is an initiative of Contemporary Art Heritage Flanders (CAHF).

Mu.ZEE

Director
Phillip Van den Bossche

Financial manager
Isabel Van Dael

Staff
Inge Busschaert, Colette Castermans, Anouck Clissen, Barbara de Jong, Huguette Devriendt, Inne Gheeraert, Sara Huycke, Els Milh, Björn Scherlippens

Technical team
Eddy Billiau, Francky Delahaye, Luc Hessens, Andy Mortier, Ronny Malesys, Kim Plasman, Lieven Stemgée, Hans Van Handenhoven, Johan Van Roose, Kathy Vercauteren, Patrick Vereecke

PUBLICATION

Concept
Phillip Van den Bossche

Editors
Mieke Mels
Björn Scherlippens

Authors
Anne Daems
Sara Huycke
Ann Veronica Janssens
Barbara de Jong
Mieke Mels
Björn Scherlippens
Ana Torfs

Transcript
Anne Catherine Roothooft
Stefan Huygebaert

Translation
Michael Meert
Robin D'hooge (text Ana Torfs)

Graphic Design
Lisa Pommerenke
Koenraad Dedobbeleer (artist insert)
Ana Torfs (case study)

Print
Stevens Print, Merelbeke

Colophon

Photography
Kristien Daem: pp. 40, 41, 43, 47, 49, 50, 51
Steven Decroos: pp. 4, 10, 13, 95 (below)
Zuzanna Ewa: pp. 94 (above)
Pieterjan Ginckels: p. 87
Dimitri Riemis: pp. 63, 73
Ana Torfs: pp. 75–83
Vandoorn Photography: p. 95 (above)
Marc Wathieu: p. 94 (below)

Special thanks to
Claudine Hellweg, Eveline Heylen, Luk Lambrecht,
Jan Op de Beeck, Stijn Punt, Els Silvrants-Barclay,
Anne Van Den Abeele, Leni Van Goidsenhoven,
Els Vermeersch.

PUBLISHER

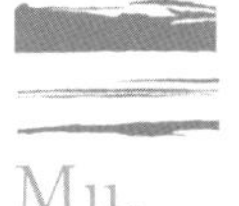

Mu.ZEE
Romestraat 11
B – 8400 Ostend
Tel. +32 (0)59 50 81 18
info@muzee.be
www.muzee.be

Mu.ZEE is an initiative of the Province of West
Flanders and the City of Ostend, and is supported
by the Flemish Community, Cobra.be, Klara, Levis,
Comitee Mu.ZEE, Kunstvaarders vzw.

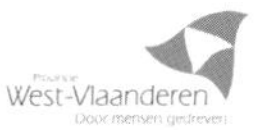
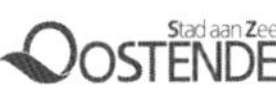
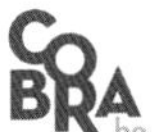
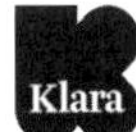
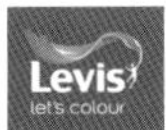
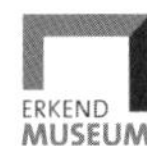
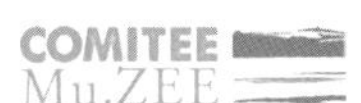
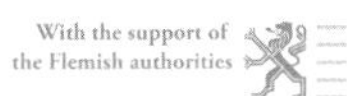

ISBN 9789081666589
D/2011/12.509/1